A 'Be Abuse Awaı
identifying differer

http://www.beab
info@beabuseaware.co.uk

"You are not obliged to accept abuse from anyone; whether they are your family, friend, or partner".

Written, published and book design by Stephen Cooke

Be Abuse Aware - Abuse
Edition 2.2

First Published - May 2021
Second Edition – March 2022

ISBN: 9798440834842

With special thanks to the contributors, and artists at www.pixabay.com for the royalty-free images used.

This book is used in conjunction with volunteers within Domestic Abuse Charities as part of their work to help individuals, professionals, and families understand what abuse is and how it is maintained. This book can also be used as a self-help study guide aimed at identifying abuse. It is not a replacement for accredited training or support from professionals and studying this with a trusted friend is recommended. An isolated incident does not indicate abuse.

Please consider making a donation to the author, donations are used to spread awareness of domestic abuse.

There are numerous charities and organizations that help with domestic abuse, some are listed towards the end of this book and the police and social services can refer you to them. Victims need to have a sense of validation regarding their feelings. Knowing the ways perpetrators employ, can help to alleviate any confusion surrounding their behavior. We hope this will increase awareness and allow more people to recognize and safeguard victims of abuse.

Society's understanding of domestic abuse is still very limited. Many emotionally healthy people simply cannot understand why a victim would put up with such behavior and some struggle to comprehend abuse that isn't physical.

Abuse is often such a vicious personal attack upon the victim, they are left mentally broken. Abuse is a process. It starts subtle and takes time for the perpetrator to wear someone down until they are isolated and dependent on their abuser (Trauma Bonded). Victims are often unable to make sense of what has happened. Confused and often traumatized, they will suffer significant harm alongside angry outbursts and acts that are completely out of their character. The Domestic Abuse Bill, sections 76 & 77 now recognizes reactive abuse (more on this later)."

Identifying and validating the abuse is pivotal for allowing victims to start the process of moving on, as well as being fully aware of what is right and wrong for the future. I hope this book will allow both victims and professionals to understand Covert and Controlling behavior. Also helping to quickly identify the difference between the victim and the perpetrator of abuse.

Written by a survivor, for survivors and professionals alike.

"Please help us to understand who is to blame!"

IMPORTANT NOTICE

Abuse and personality disorders are all perceived as a scale from good to bad. Some traits are considered healthy at one end, and abusive at the other. Never self diagnose yourself or others, always consult a professional and never try to deal with abusers yourself.

This book is meant as information only and is not a substitute for professional help. Many IDVA's, Social Services, police and Domestic Abuse Support workers will be more than willing to help. Including your local council who have domestic abuse coordinators who can assist you.

Contents

What is **Abuse**?

Chapter 1 - Introduction

Coercive abuse makes life very confusing for victims. Abuse can be physical, psychological, emotional, sexual, financial, or social abuse. In law, Domestic Abuse is defined as being in an intimate or family relationship. Victims will have endured profound anguish and trauma often leading to severe mental health problems and working memory problems. In this book I will attempt to familiarise you with not just abuse, but the terms generally used in the identification of abuse.

Abusive is a means of gaining power and control over another person. By gradually wearing them down and pushing against the victims boundaries. Molding their victim into conforming to their ideals. As a result, victims become a shadow of their former selves, unable to perform simple self-care routines for fear of being attacked verbally or physically. Coercion is making another party act in an involuntary manner – under duress – by the use of threats, lies, or force.

Statistics indicate that women make up 85% of the victims of domestic abuse (Kershaw et al 2008). Domestic abuse is generally seen as both a cause and consequence of gender inequalities in society. However, it is important to recognize that anyone can experience domestic abuse, regardless of their gender, age, race, ethnic, religious group, class, sexuality, disability, or lifestyle. The government's definition of domestic abuse has recently been extended to include anyone over the age of 16 within the Domestic Abuse bill 2021. In the past, it covered people aged 18+.

I spent 25 years in an abusive marriage. I did not even realise it was abuse until it was over, it is common to not have the experience to understand what is happening. Abusers will often use intimidation, threats and project their own wrongdoing onto others. When someone starts to realise they are a victim of domestic abuse, they will try to 'fix' things or apply boundaries in an attempt to stop or reduce the abuse. The abuser then reacts to this. They may threaten to hurt you or those in your care in order to maintain their control. During this phase of enlightening, it is vitally important to have a support network in place. It is far more desirable to remove yourself or the victim from the abuser's control completely. This is nearly always the professionals preferred approach.

Domestic abuse is different for everyone and alongside the acts of violence that cause physical harm, many victims will also experience verbal abuse, name-calling, habitual criticism, insults, yelling (raging), and shaming. Abusers are experts at the use of underhanded emotional manipulation tactics that the victim may not be aware of. This is a covert and intentional method of psychological warfare. The abuser does see their victim as an enemy – I personally like to say "If you want a quick idea of what someone is like, watch how they treat their enemies".

Abusing by proxy is when the perpetrator of abuse will gain the help of a mutual friend, family member, or simple manipulation of a third party, to help them continue the abuse of the victim. A newer term circulating on social media which is used to describe this type of behaviour is **'flying monkeys'.** This is normally done by telling others how 'bad' the victim is, often portraying the victim as the abuser.

Many 'flying monkeys' believe the abuser and could may believe they are trying to help. But it can also be the case, that they are actually aware and either enjoying the 'drama' or are simply siding with the abuser. In families the old saying blood is thicker than water is often used as an excuse to justify the abusers behaviour. These types of families are especially dangerous as they will encourage (either consciously or subconsciously) the abusive behavior. In abuse, it is not always the case that both parties have some responsibility in arguments, "it takes two" is a type of victim shaming and not just misleading but actually cause more harm than good. In an abusive relationship, it is common for only the perpetrator to be at fault. Reactions to abuse, even extreme reactions are trauma responses **(Reactive Abuse)** and should be handled as such.

It's very important to realise the difference between reactive abuse and the perpetrators' abuse. Often their are excuses reasons behind the abuse, such as childhood trauma, being drunk, or having a bad day. These causes cannot be used as an excuse for the perpetrator's behavior, their behavior stems from a need to control and dominate their partners. You may even find yourself excusing abuse based on the past of the perpetrator. While these underlying causes can be examined to help understand the behavior, they cannot be used to justify it. Abuse is rarely caused by a lack of self-control and often is a deliberate choice that is made. Remember their public face is a friendly and charming one, most of the time.

Chapter 2 - Behaviours associated with potential abuse

Many of us show behaviours which could be identified as abusive, especially on bad days. But these are not deal breakers and one or two doesn't guarantee that a partner will become abusive. We all have our flaws, no one is perfect.

However, an increase in new abusive behaviours or an increase in intensity should never be ignored. The following attributes are what is called **Red flags,** but people who show them are not necessarily abusers. Frequently showing these behaviours however, or carrying them to the extreme should be viewed as potential abusive behaviour.

- Past Patterns of abuse.

- Aggression during sex or playful use of force during sexuality.

- Cruelty to animals and children.

- Rude to strangers.

- Consistent blame & bullying.

- Hypersensitivity.

- Concern as control.

- Jealousy.

- moving to quickly.

- Alcohol or substance abuse.

- Controlling behavior & Isolation.

- Lying.

- Cheating.

- Constantly fighting or thinking that 'fighting' is a good night out.

More information on red flags can be found in chapter 24.

Chapter 3 - Physical Abuse.

Physical abuse   WIKIPEDIA
                                                  The Free Encyclopedia
From Wikipedia, the free encyclopedia

[1]**Physical abuse** is any intentional act causing injury or trauma to another person or animal by way of bodily contact. In most cases, children are the victims of physical abuse, but adults can also be victims, as in cases of domestic violence or workplace aggression. Alternative terms sometimes used include physical assault or physical violence, and may also include sexual abuse. Physical abuse may involve more than one abuser, and more than one victim.

Physical abuse can include many different types of assault. They may physically hit their victim or punch, kick, spit or slap! Some abuser's will use more serious types of assault, such as strangling and burning as well as physically restraining, pushing, pulling hair and/or using weapons.

In the Domestic Abuse bill 2021, it clearly states that violence or abuse against a partner for the sexual gratification of either party is not a defense when brought to court. These types of assaults do often increase in severity over time and the more the abuser is allowed to inflict his/her abuse, the more long term damage can be caused.

Simply allowing the perpetrator to get away with bad behaviour, simply to keep the peace and 'not cause an argument' will have the effect over time of increasing their abusive behaviour in nearly all circumstances. Medical studies have also identified domestic abuse as a factor in serious brain injuries (Corrigan et al 2003) as well as physical injuries such as broken bones and bruising (Campbell 2002).

Perpetrators of abuse may also 'demonstrate' their physical dominance by punching walls and furniture or assaulting pets and other family members. Abusers often behave in a hostile, loud and "in your face", aggressive manner to intimate and force your compliance. Victims can feel like any argument could be their last. Arguments can be healthy and are a normal part of any relationship. They are used to resolve issues, but abusers will make it very clear that negative conversations will not just jeopardize the relationship but may actually result in the victim being punished. Once the cause of the argument has been settled, giving each other space and privacy is normal. Abusers expect you to be happy and loving straight after which is not always possible. With covert abuse it's not always obvious that domestic abuse is present. If this is suspected, never disregard it.

There are various signs of physical abuse, it's important to note here that in most cases, physical abuse is often done to parts of the body not visible to others. Physical abuse is different from defending yourself or reacting.

Physical abuse includes;

Bruises (particularly if the individual can not be clear about how the bruising happened). The most obvious are on the face. Black eyes or bruised cheeks.

Broken bones. Survivors of physical abuse who experience broken bones may have a history of more than one broken bone. X-rays will likely show fractures or breaks in various stages of healing.

Burns. This is a common type of physical abuse. Cigarette burns, burns or blisters from scalding water or grease burns that cover a large area of the body, hand burns from hobs or naked flames.

Head injuries. A concussion is a common sign of physical abuse. Again being evasive about how the injury occurred could be a warning sign.

Questions?

1. What other signs of physical violence can you think of?
2. How could someone hide the signs of abuse?
3. What would raise your own suspicions that someone was not being truthful and hiding their injuries?
4. Who would you tell if you had concerns about abuse?

Chapter 4 - Rage and the Cycle of Abuse.

Cycle of abuse

From Wikipedia, the free encyclopedia

The **cycle of abuse** is a social cycle theory developed in 1979 by Lenore E. Walker to explain patterns of behavior in an abusive relationship. The phrase is also used more generally to describe any set of conditions which perpetuate abusive and dysfunctional relationships, such as in poor child rearing practices which tend to get passed down. Walker used the term more narrowly, to describe the cycling patterns of calm, violence, and reconciliation within an abusive relationship. Critics suggest the theory was based on inadequate research criteria, and cannot therefore be generalized upon.

The rage of an abuser is often referred to as **'narcissistic rage'** on social media. This rage is often directed at the victim, but is a projection of the abusers mood and confusion on the inside. The arguments of an abuser can last from hours to days before calming down. This rage was documented and **the Cycle of Abuse** is a theory developed by Lenore Walker in her book, The battered Woman from 1979. This cycle is similar to **the power and control wheel** described later. The Cycle of abuse is described as having four stages: Tension Building, Incident, Reconciliation and Calm. Each stage is defined by certain characteristics.

Tension-Building. This is the stage where the abuser is triggered and his/her tension builds. It could have nothing to do with the victim and include stresses of daily life, work, bills or conflict over ex partners or children. Again there are deeper concerns such as the risk factors in domestic abuse covered later.

Incident. This phase is where the incidents of explosive rage or violence, emotional, psychological or other forms of abuse erupt. The perpetrator will use any elements he can think of to control and dominate his victim. Often (but not all the while) using anger and/or violent outbursts and projecting anything they could do themselves onto the victim. Abusers will often blame the victim for wrongs they have thought about doing themselves.

Reconciliation. This is where the rage has calmed down and the abuser will start to make excuses and apologies, often called the 'honeymoon' period. Often showing remorse and begging for forgiveness they blame anyone and anything for their reactions. Promising this will never happen again, that they will seek help and even try to blame the victim for provoking their actions, diminishing and sweeping under the carpet everything that has happened during the incident or the extent of the harm that was caused. Gaslighting is often massively engaged at this point.

www.beabuseaware.org

16

Calm. This is the time when things are relatively calm and peaceful. Love-bombing is used and the abuser may even carry out some of the promises to seek help or change. As time goes on the abuser however falls back into the cycle, showing less and less effort in their behavior and the demands and stresses of everyday life begin the tension-building phase again.

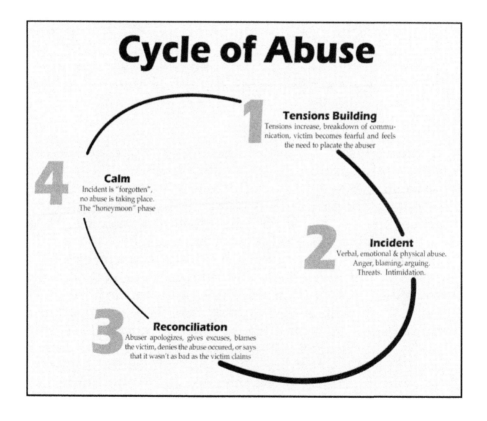

Chapter 5 - Emotional & Psychological Abuse.

Where physical abuse often leaves physical evidence, emotional abuse tends to be more hidden, subtle, and a far more sophisticated form of domestic abuse. It far harder to recognize and take legal action against. Through this type of abuse abusers can erode the identity of any victim, often victims are highly intelligent, capable and confident. These characteristics are generally the traits abusers aim for. The intentions of the abuser are the same as other types of domestic abuse because they are seeking to control, degrade, humiliate and punish the victim. Emotional and physiological abuse can cause lasting trauma. These effects cannot be minimized because they affect a person's everyday life to such an extent normal day to day tasks can become impossible. Often memory lapses and confusion are signs of this trauma. It is very common for emotional abuse to include the use of threats; for instance a perpetrator may threaten to take the children or report the victim to Social Services as an unfit parent, threaten to or actually harm a family member if the victim leaves or says that they will kill themselves if the relationship ends.

It is also extremely common for the perpetrators' control over their victims to continue well after any physical separation. It's important to understand that healing can only start when this influence is no longer present.

Read these examples;

- I will report you to the police.
- I will report you to Social Services.
- I will report you to the Benefits agency.
- I will tell 'someone' about how you're abusing me.
- 'Someone' is going to beat you up or kill you.
- I will not let you have any money.
- I will tell others you're lying about 'something'.
- I will make your kids hate you.
- I will take your kids away from you.
- I will tell everyone you hit me.
- I will tell everyone your crazy so no one will believe you.
- I will make you homeless.
- I will stop you from seeing your friends or family.
- I will destroy this family.
- I will have you committed (to a mental hospital).
- If you post something about you on 'social media' I will make trouble/drama or argue.
- I will embarrass you in public.
- Telling you to comply or there is 'no telling what I will do'.
- I will hurt the children unless you do this.
- If you do that, then I will hurt the children.

Have any of these been used against you personally? **Gaslighting** is talked about more in Chapter 13.

Perpetrators will try to isolate the victim as a form of control. This will include friends and family by 'discouraging' them from going out or contacting family and friends. This is sometimes done by attacking the integrity and character of friends and family or arguing over the smallest of things to 'punish' you subconsciously for even daring to have your own life. Your hobbies or even work are very often discouraged and the sense of choice and control you have is undermined because you are often excluded from making important decisions. There are some signs to watch for when a person has or is suffering emotional abuse.

Some of these are;

- The person feels afraid to speak their mind.
- They hate asking for help.
- They bury their emotions.
- They view their own needs as a burden.
- They need everything to be perfect.
- They feel ignored if they do speak up.
- They have a harsh inner critic.
- Any form of criticism is triggering and overwhelming.

TASK.

For each of the following, give 3 examples of how perpetrators would achieve their goal;

1. Isolation,
2. Making jokes that are actually insulting,
3. Catastrophism (Making a mountain out of a molehill!),
4. Guilt Tripping.

Chapter 7 - Love-Bombing

Love bombing

From Wikipedia, the free encyclopedia

Love bombing is an attempt to influence a person by demonstrations of attention and affection. It happens when someone overwhelms the victim with loving words or physical actions with manipulative behaviours.[1] It can be used in different ways and for either positive or negative purposes.[2] Psychologists have identified love bombing as a possible part of a cycle of abuse and have warned against it. Critics of cults use the phrase with the implication that the "love" is feigned and that the practice is psychological manipulation in order to create a feeling of unity within the group against a society perceived as hostile[3] In 2011 clinical psychologist Oliver James advocated love bombing in his book *Love Bombing: Reset Your Child's Emotional Thermostat*, as a means for parents to rectify emotional problems in their children.[4]

When a relationship with an abuser starts, it's common for things to move extremely fast. Abusers can already have a lot of information about you from social media or friends. For instance what you have in common, your likes, dislikes and where you like to go. This is how they pretend to be perfect for their victim. Doing this they mirror the victims hopes, dreams and past hurt. Using their insecurities and loneliness to form an immediate bond of trust. They may be very overwhelming and initiate communication on every level, flooding your social media or texts with love, poems, songs, compliments, and inside jokes to put off penitential suitors.

Abusers also have an endless list of pity plays and sob stories for them both to bond over. Often abusers don't know themselves what they actually want, they will make a massive point of telling you their good traits, not letting you spot them on your own.

Abusers say drama is not their thing, but often there's more drama around them than anywhere else. **Love-bombing** is the **Idealisation** phase of the abuse cycle. Often used at the beginning of a relationship or when they feel they are losing control of the victim. This person who victims fall for, the cute and charming person does not actually exist. This persona they use is soon replaced by something else entirely. The victim may even be scared by the emotional emptiness of the 'devil eyes', the cold manipulative, and the inconsiderate things that slips through the mask. The victim will feel something isn't right but won't be able to put their finger on it until much later.

Do you think there are any tell-tale signs you could look out for when forming a new relationship? Read the following **Red Flags** and see how many you can add. There is more about dating abuse and red flags in chapter 23.

These can be very difficult to spot if you are unaware.

www.beabuseaware.org

1. They have cheated on a past partner,

2. They push your boundaries in 'innocent' ways,

3. They rush a new relationship far too quickly,

4. They try to isolate you from friends and family,

5. They hold you to double standards,

6. All their previous partners are 'crazy',

7. They call you names in arguments,

8. They make you feel confused or stupid,

9. They cannot stop saying just how perfect you are,

10. They refuse to work, without a reason,

11. They're cruel to their parents or strangers,

12. There secretive about things,

13. They demand to have your passwords and phone,

14. They guilt trip you every chance they get,

15. They make fun of you,

16. They 'roll' their eyes at you a lot,

17. They refuse to make your relationship public,

18. Their mood can change in an instant,

19. They're incapable of saying sorry.

Chapter 8 - Trauma Bonding/Stockholm Syndrome

Trauma bonding or **_Stockholm Syndrome_** is a victims response they may have to an abuser to keep the relationship going. Stockholm Syndrome is widely recognised in the context of hostages and captors, but also happens within abusive relationships.

A lot of professionals consider this a coping mechanism of dealing with the trauma of domestic abuse, hence trauma bonding.

Trauma bonding victims sympathise with their abuser, develop feelings and trust them. Often due to the **mirroring** of the victim they share common goals. Abusers quickly isolate the victim, building a distrust of friends, family and even the police. This is increased when they are also reliant on the abuser.

Stockholm syndrome develops because people are placed in a situation where they feel intense fear of harm and believe all control is in the hands of their tormentor. Trauma bonding includes sympathy and support for their abusers plight and may even manifest in negative feelings toward officers who are trying to help the victims. Actual situations in which the victims have displayed this kind of response have included hostage situations, long-term kidnappings, Domestic Abuse, members of cults, prisoners of concentration camps, and more.

Stockholm syndrome requires specialist counseling.

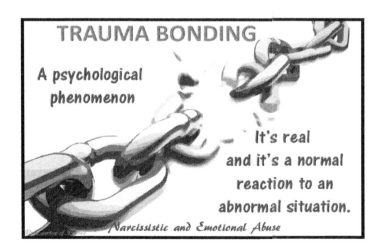

Image Credit: http://narcissisticandemotionalabuse.co.uk/

Often people with Trauma bonding also have other mental health problems such as **depression**. **Anxiety** and **C-PTS** is also an issue. The way that victims are treated can vary between relationships. Trauma bonding is complex and further reading is recommend. The following example

One emotional technique the perpetrator uses is being highly critical of the victim. They will blatantly call you names such as 'stupid', 'loser', 'lazy', or other words much too offensive to put into text. The perpetrator becomes not only the giver of the abuse but also able to take away the abuse or protect you from the abuse. They are able to prevent the threatened action if you do as you're told.

The passive/aggressive cycle used to achieve this trauma bond is easy to miss due to the confusion it creates. One minute they will shower you with attention, another they will ignore you or criticize you. Of course, the 'public' image is always maintained and they will treat you differently in public than behind closed doors.

Abusers will actively put in as little effort as possible and only engage more when you try to disengage. Spotting all these signs early on will prevent the victim from falling into another abusive relationship out of the need to be accepted. Trauma bonding leaves a lasting impression almost like a drug dependency and unless treated as such, victims are doomed to repeat abusive relationships because being abused feels familiar, feelings that are familiar make you feel safe.

Abusive relationships are very often one-sided. 'It takes two to tango', or 'you must have done something to deserve it' shames the victim and can become another form of abuse. The dominant traits of an abusive relationship are control and power. The perpetrator wants complete control over the victim. It is widely believed the 'mask' of Mr Nice guy will slip in around 6 months or less of contact. If the victim develops a bond as a coping mechanism (also remember most abusers are not 100% abusive, 100% of the time), they will often remember this 'loving' bond and start accepting the abuse because they want to get this loving and caring person back.

The Power and Control Wheel was developed by the Domestic Violence Intervention program in Minnesota, US, and is now widely used throughout the world in helping victims of domestic abuse to highlight the tactics used by abusers.

The Power and Control Wheel

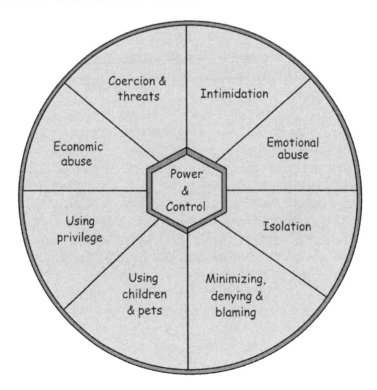

Chapter 9 - Character assassination, and Circular Conversations.

Bullying! Its extremely common for abusers to use derogatory names or 'character assassination' techniques.

Character assassination

From Wikipedia, the free encyclopedia

WIKIPEDIA
The Free Encyclopedia

Character assassination (CA) is a deliberate and sustained effort to damage the reputation or credibility of an individual.[1] The term could also be selectively applied to social groups and institutions. Agents of character assassinations employ a mix of open and covert methods to achieve their goals, such as raising false accusations, planting and fostering rumors, and manipulating information.

Character assassination happens through character attacks. These can take many forms, such as spoken insults, speeches, pamphlets, campaign ads, cartoons, and internet memes. As a result of character attacks, individuals may be rejected by their professional community or members of their social or cultural environment. For some historical figures, that damage endures for centuries.

CA may involve exaggeration, misleading half-truths, or manipulation of facts to present an untrue picture of the targeted person. It is a form of defamation and can be a form of *ad hominem* argument.

The phrase "character assassination" became popular from around 1930.[2] This concept, as a subject of scholarly study, was originally introduced by Davis (1950)[3] in his collection of essays revealing the dangers of political smear campaigns. Six decades later Icks and Shiraev (2014)[1] rejuvenated the term and revived academic interest by addressing and comparing a variety of historical character assassination events.

Character assassination is when your personality, confidence and self esteem are damaged by another. Have you ever been called "my dumpling" or an ape? Made to feel undermined and not a good person. It is difficult to know in all circumstances if these terms are meant as simple banter – if you have told them it hurts your feelings, then it should stop. If it doesn't then it's very possible these comments can be emotional abuse. Yelling is also an extremely effective method of control and emotional abuse. Screaming, swearing or raging as I like to say, are meant to intimidate while making the victim feel worthless and small – it's often accompanied by fist-pounding, temper tantrums or throwing/breaking things. The more subtle character assassination is done in a number of ways such as eye-rolling, smirking, head shaking or telling you that this 'subject' is just beyond your understanding.

An abuser will dismiss their actions when confronted about them. Calling them a 'joke' and attempting to make you look foolish for reacting. Comparing the victim to others in their life such as ex-lovers, friends, or their family to **devalue** and make the victim feel jealous and inferior. After the love bombing phase, the qualities the abuser once claimed they loved, have now become glaring faults and the victim will try and address these, spending more and more time trying to prove they are the very same person as the abuser once 'fell in love with. Always remember that an abuser's weapon of choice is **Narcissistic word salad!** This is different from the clinical definition of Word Salad.

The narcissistic word salad is a verbal assassination.

The term "word salad" refers to a circular language tactic used by one individual to ensure that talks never end positively for the other. It is a technique for exerting influence over another person's views or ideas, emotional response, or access to information.

www.beabuseaware.org

Just when you think you have something worked out, you're forced to begin discussing it again in two minutes! Reciting everything that has already been said. The abuser uses the same garbage and random arguments and ignores any legitimate arguments or concerns you have.

The resolution will be on their terms only, and if you have genuine worries such as why they're on the phone, why they're eager to get off the phone when you're there and you bring this up. It will be like you have never talked about it before. They will make you feel crazy or high maintenance and blame you, saying they're sick of arguing about this. It's basically a conversation from hell. They will throw one thing after another at you, not actually saying anything, but talking at you.

These circular arguments will have your head spinning and can cause serious anxiety and damage to your self esteem! Disengage as much as you can. Once you realise they are doing this, there is little that can be done if there not willing to see where the problem lies and all you can do is protect your well-being.

The grey rock method is when you appear boring when interacting with abusive or manipulative people. The term "grey rock" refers to how you become unresponsive, similar to a rock.

avoiding interactions with the abusive person.

keeping unavoidable interactions brief.

giving short or one-word answers to questions.

communicating in a factual, unemotional way.

The aim is to cause the abusive person to lose interest and stop their abusive behavior.

www.beabuseaware.org

If you point out something they're doing, they'll start recounting the numerous unrelated things that you have done wrong in the past. Then using these to compare their actions to yours. "My cheating isn't as bad as what you did!", or "you can't complain about it because".

It is very hard and time-consuming going through this type of situation, you could go hours or days replaying the argument, obsessing over it only to have the whole thing bought up again the next time the abuser is in a mood.

This repeated behaviour slowly and steadily erodes away any boundaries the victim had. Abusers groom you into accepting their bad behaviour as the 'norm'. Teasing becomes the primary mode of communication in the relationship. Victim's learn to push away their feelings to 'keep the peace', in essence becoming numb. The victim will constantly be on edge, walking on eggshells around the abuser.

This traumatic situation will keep the victim in a state of fight or flight, also known as hyper-arousal or an acute stress response. It's very common for the victim to try and come up with a diplomatic solution, where the blame is often split between the parties so you can both apologize while the abuser saves face. Victims of domestic abuse will often find they are the ones doing all the apologizing.

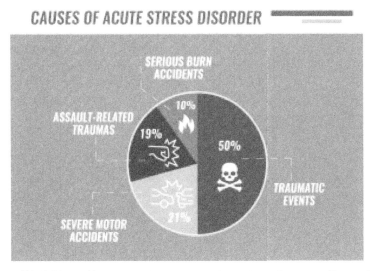

Credit: https://www.stress.org/acute-stress-disorder

Accomplishments, interests and minimisation.

Minimisation (psychology)

From Wikipedia, the free encyclopedia
(Redirected from Belittle)

Minimisation or **minimization** is a type of deception[1] involving denial coupled with rationalisation/rationalization in situations where complete denial is implausible. It is the opposite of exaggeration. Minimisation, or downplaying the significance of an event or emotion, is a common strategy in dealing with feelings of guilt.[2] Words associated with minimisation include:

Always remember, you are important. No-one has the right to insult your appearance, say your hair is ugly or your outfit horrible! These types of insults are again aimed at undermining your self image, your choices and ultimately your control. Perpetrators will belittle your accomplishments and say your achievements mean nothing, often claiming responsibility for any success you have. "I made you, I can destroy you" is a quote often used. They will put down your interests saying they are worthless, stupid and a waste of time. They could say they are out of your league, even telling you they are protecting you from looking stupid. Be fully aware, perpetrators will know what annoys you, and they will bring it up again and again any chance they get.

They might try to embarrass you in public or in front of friends and will lecture you in front of others about all the things you do wrong or have outbursts in public.

"Never allow someone else to tell you how to feel, or who you are!" Often an abuser will provoke jealousy or rivalries while maintaining their own innocence. After the love-bombing phase where they have been directing all their attention towards the victim, it can be very confusing when they withdraw and focus on someone else. After such a beautiful and emotionally focused start to the relationship these rivalries are encouraged because of the need for "supplying the drama" abusers crave.

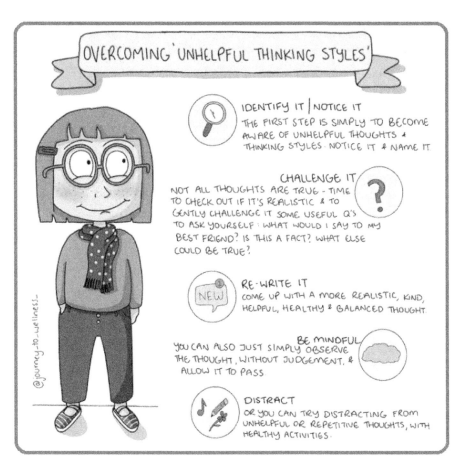

Monitoring, Spying, and financial control.

PASSWORDS

Passwords are the biggest risk abusers often get access to information because they know or can guess a password.

Here are some top tips for passwords:

1. Don't use obvious security questions
2. Create different passwords for different accounts
3. Download a password manager software or use suggested passwords
4. Activate 2FA - Two Factor Authentication, this is an extra layer of security for online accounts and often includes using an App or text message code to log in.
5. Don't use pet names or special dates, using a nonsense phrase is far more secure.
6. Do not reuse passwords
7. Be careful filling out social media games asking for personal information such as pet names, birthdays, or other information you might have used in a password
8. Change passwords frequently

BAA | B E
A B U S E
A W A R E | www.BeAbuseAware.co.uk
Challenge abuse by gaining knowledge and learning what FREE resources are available.

It is often the case with abusive relationships which are 'toxic' that monitoring your whereabouts is a real issue. They will want to know where you are at all times. Insist that you respond to calls and texts immediately and might even show up where you're supposed to be. This is controlling behaviour. It may be they act like this for a reason other than being controlling or abusive, such as they have been abused themselves in the past, cheated on, abandoned or lost a loved one.

If their behaviour is causing you to be unhappy, scared or isolated then this is a problem that needs addressing. Often this monitoring will include digital means such as checking your internet history, emails or texts. Going as far as demanding your passwords and if you don't tell them accusing you of hiding something just so you comply to prove your innocence. This is unacceptable and is abuse. Controlling the victims' banking, not allowing them their own accounts, or having to ask permission to spend your own money is abuse. If they cancel appointments without your knowledge and say others canceled them, that is abuse. Speaking with your work boss and colleagues without you knowing, telling them about your habits, or causing issues with your ability to socialize with them can also be abuse.

SPYWARE

You won't know it's installed!

Antivirus software won't work!

Spyware is malicious software that a partner or anyone who has access to your phone or computer, could install on your equipment that collects information on everything you do online as well as recording passwords all without your knowledge.

If you suspect spyware, perform a factory reset on your phones and tablets, reinstall your trusted apps and remember to backup your personal photos and information. Don't clone copy as this could also copy the spyware.

For Laptops and Desktops, go to www.safer-networking.org and download and run there FREE software Spybot 'search and destroy'.

Afterwards - change all your passwords and security questions

BAA | B E
A B U S E
A W A R E | www.BeAbuseAware.co.uk
Challenge abuse by gaining knowledge and
learning what FREE resources are available.

Have you ever been 'ordered' to do something?

My way or the highway
From Wikipedia, the free encyclopedia

WIKIPEDIA
The Free Encyclopedia

For other uses, see My way or the highway (disambiguation).

My way or the highway is a predominantly American idiom that dates back to the 1970s.[1] It suggests an ultimatum like "take it or leave it", which indicates that the listener(s) (who are typically not in a position to challenge the options, e.g. employees or those lacking money) must totally accept the speaker's decision or suffer negative consequences such as being fired, asked to leave, or receive nothing. The idiom literally tells the listener that if they don't wish to follow the speaker's demands they will have to leave, specifically, go take the highway out of town, otherwise, if they choose to stay, they will be required to follow the speaker's demands. The idiom may sometimes be seen with other pronouns, for example, **her way or the highway**.

Directly ordering you to do something, such as "get my dinner done, now", "make me a cup of tea" or "Stop taking the pill" are often expected to be followed without question by the abuser. When you do question them, even if you have plans to the contrary then the rage and abuse can start. Often lasting long after you have given in and just done as you're told. This type of abuse is meant as a punishment, they will often use condescending and patronizing tones almost as if mocking you. They will raise their eyebrows, smirk, argue, become physical, scream or feign disappointment!

Abusers do not recognize that you do have the right to refuse or have your own **boundaries**, their needs come first and if they don't they brand you selfish. Often you are then treated like a child or end up being on the receiving end of having long conversations about how helpless they are, how much they need and rely on you.

They simply cannot live without you.

When you do try to stick up for yourself, respecting your boundaries it often results in rages. These are a terrible sight to behold, its almost unbelievable that a grown adult can act this way! Abusers who have personality disorders are very unpredictable and often their rages occur at any time and over small things. These rages have a common connection. Control, power, and shame. It is believed that some people with personality disorders are incapable of feeling more than one strong emotion at a time.

During arguments, abusers will bring up every incidence they can think of! It will all be up for debate, even if it occurred last year or 20 years ago. The list of outrageous accusations these types of personalities can accuse you of, in my opinion can actually be a projection of what they can do, or would do if they are in your situation. Often using others to help them gain an advantage. Never be fooled into thinking they are 'only joking'. If you have told them you don't like something, it hurts you or upsets you, then it's not a joke and it's become a weapon.

To abusers arguments are competitions and they do not like to lose.

Gaslighting.

Gaslighter's will blatantly deny they are manipulating the victim, even ignoring evidence when confronted with it.

Gaslighter's will not address their bad behavior, instead, it will always be made out to be your fault! You're too 'sensitive' or you're 'crazy'. They are the definition of hypocrites, having extremely high morals which their victims must stick to, but they are free to do anything they wish. In relationships where abuse is present, there is often an imbalance of power. You will find yourself apologizing without knowing what you did wrong.

Gaslighting is when one person intentionally distorts reality, using lies and misinformation to get their warped reality believed. Victims often question their sanity, perception of reality and memories.

Perpetrators will deceive their victim, consciously most of the time their actions could be due to a lack of emotional intelligence or understanding but this is rare and often they will have a per-diagnosed condition. Gaslighters systematically chip away at the victim, leaving them feeling confused, anxious, and unable to trust themselves. Read this section carefully to fully understand Gaslighting effects and how to protect yourself from this horrendous form of abuse.

The recounted excuses below may seem so familiar to you, the same old promises will never match the actions. It's normal for the victim to find themselves playing detective, even if they have never done so in any other relationship. They are seeking answers to a feeling they can't explain, then can actually start feeling bad and start thinking they are being abusive.

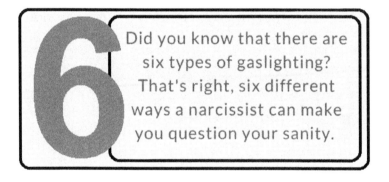
Did you know that there are six types of gaslighting? That's right, six different ways a narcissist can make you question your sanity.

"Jane is home alone, she locks the front door and goes upstairs. John returns home, unlocks the front door then starts an argument with Jane for leaving the front door unlocked."

The following are some signs and examples of gaslighting, the end result, conscious or not, is to make the other person doubt their own sanity by manipulation of the facts giving the gaslighter the feeling of power and control over their victim.

Signs of gaslighting can include;

- A focus on your own character flaws,
- Self-esteem is at rock bottom,
- Second-guessing yourself all the while,
- You often feel confused,
- You find it hard or impossible to make decisions,
- Saying sorry all the while,
- Feeling like a disappointment,
- A feeling of disconnection from your past self,
- Making excuses for the Gaslighters behavior,
- You lie to yourself to avoid confusion,
- You believe, or are told you are too sensitive,
- You are tense around the gas-lighter,
- You have a sense of something is wrong, but cannot put your finger on it,
- You feel trapped and cannot see any way out.

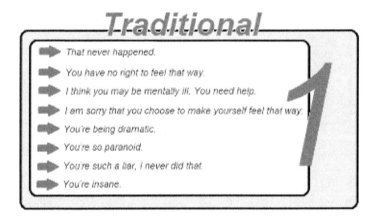

The following is information around Gaslighting. Remember, these character traits do not just exist in films! they exist in abusers as well!

1. Blatant lying

Characters who use gaslighting tell obvious and lies, unnecessary and even tiny lies. You know that they are lying. The issue is how they are lying with such ease. The gaslighter is setting you up in an abusive pattern. You begin to question everything around you, and become uncertain of the simplest matters and of yourself. This self-doubt is exactly what the gaslighter wants.

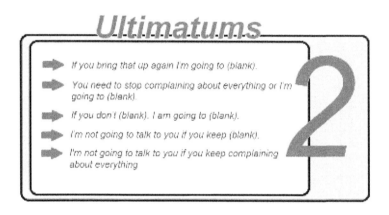

2. Deny, Deny, Deny

Again, you know exactly what they have said. However, they completely deny saying it. Sometimes victim's go as far as to record the conversations in an attempt to self validate or prove to their abuser that, they are in fact, the abuser! (Legally recordings can be classed as 'abusive' behavior) The gaslighter often asks them to 'prove it,' knowing that, in some situations you only have your memory of the conversation.

This results in the victim questioning their memory and their reality. Abusers will deny what happened knowing full well the victim is in the right, from the start they face a losing battle and are further traumatized just attempting to get to the truth! The abuser's enablers (**flying monkeys**) will back up their side of the story, often because they have been pre-warned about how crazy the victim is, want to stick up for the abuse anyway or they simply enjoy the drama and the chance to "get at" the victim. They may even be under the misguided idea they are trying to help you.

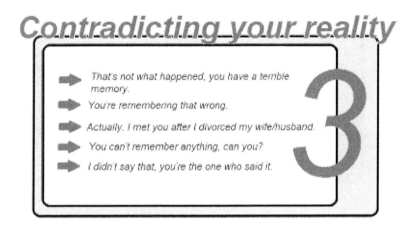

Contradicting your reality

➡ That's not what happened, you have a terrible memory.

➡ You're remembering that wrong.

➡ Actually, I met you after I divorced my wife/husband.

➡ You can't remember anything, can you?

➡ I didn't say that, you're the one who said it.

3

3. Using what you love against you

Abusers will use what is closest to you, against you. If you love your job, they will find issues with it, not enough pay, working around the opposite sex, bad influence, etc. If you have children, the gaslighter may force you to believe you should never have had them, should punish them more, or become jealous of the time you spend with them forcing you to choose between them. This abusive manipulation tactic causes the victim to question the foundation of themselves as well as what they hold close to their heart.

4. The slow death of the victim

One of the terrifying parts of gaslighting is the methodical timeline that the abuser uses. The manipulation happens gradually over time. This has the victim morphing into someone entirely different. The most confident human being can become a shell of a person without even being aware of it. The victim's individual reality disintegrates around them and can result in the victim subconsciously copying the abusive traits of the abuser.

5. Words vs. Actions

Notably, a person who gaslights talks and talks. They can be extremely convincing because they have had a lot of practice! However, their words mean nothing. Therefore, it is important to look at what they are doing. The issues lie in their abusive actions towards the victim.

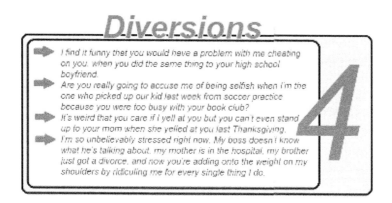

6. Love and flattery

A common technique of a person who gaslights is to tear you down and then build you back up (the cycle of abuse). The uneasiness the victim feels is because without realizing, they are becoming used to being torn down. However, the praise may lead you to think that the abuser isn't all that bad. The victim often begins to crave this praise which can and does lead to codependency.

7. Confusion

Without a doubt, everyone craves stability. The gaslighter knows this, and the constant confusion that the abuser has instilled leads the victim to become desperate for clarity. More often than not, the victim searches for this clarity in the abuser, trying to heal or help them at first. But finally just trying to make sense of something which cannot be made sense of, thus continuing the cycle of abuse and increasing the power that the abuser has. This confusion often leads to actual memory loss and confusion.

8. Projecting

The abuser's traits of being a liar and a cheater are often hidden apart from those who they abuse. They will believe the victim is capable of the same despicable acts and will accuse you of being the liar and the cheater. You constantly feel like you need to defend yourself for things you haven't done or need to. The abuser will even accuse you of the things they would 'want to' or be 'capable' of doing. Things any normal person could not even get their heads around! In the end the only way to understand an abuser – is to stop understanding them.

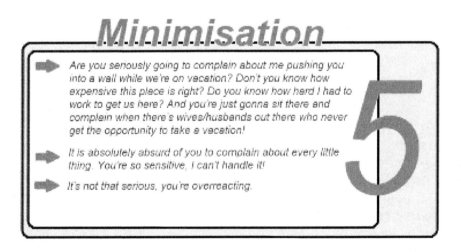

9. "You're crazy"

The gaslighter will know you are questioning your sanity. The gaslighter also knows that you come to them trying to make sense of it all, but they are purposefully causing the confusion. So when you are trying to make sense of things, and they call you crazy and the abuser, you might actually believe it. Furthermore, the gaslighter may tell others such as family, friends, or work colleagues that you're crazy or abusive. This way if you were ever to approach them for help, they wouldn't believe you. This 'heads up' the abuser has given your mutual friends, claiming that this would happen will reinforce the idea that you're too "crazy" to be taken seriously.

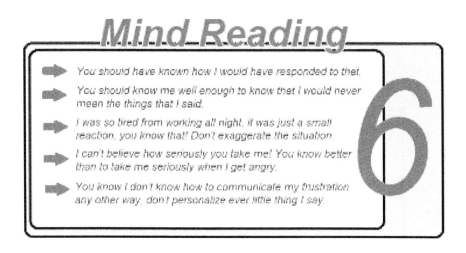

10. Everyone else is a liar

The abuser may also instill in you the fear that everyone else is against you and others are all liars, you can only trust in them forcing your sense of reality to be further blurred. People who gaslight want the control over the victim, that way the victim only has them to turn to for everything. This allows the abuse to continue.

Gaslighting can only be described as a weapon, it aims to degrade someone's mental state making them vulnerable to control or suggestion. The quicker a victim can pick up on these gaslighting techniques, the better you can protect yourself – this is where a strong support network of family and friends is essential. Not mutual friends, or only the abuser's friends, but having distinct individual friends you can turn to for advice.

Gaslighting is a clear form of psychological abuse and actively employed by Narcissists, cult leaders, dictators, and abusers seeking power and control. People who suffer from the **Dark Triad** personality disorders use gaslighting extensively.

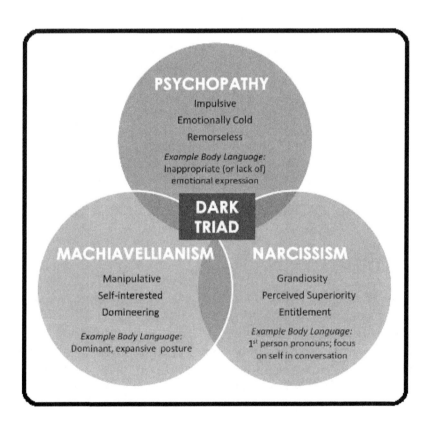

I do love bullet points, They are straight to the point and easy to read! The following are examples of gaslighting, learn to recognise the signs.

- If you continue to question me like I'm a criminal, I'm going to ACT like one.
- You realize without him/her you'd be a nobody.
- I am ignoring you because I don't want to argue/hit you.
- You never listen!
- You need to grow up!
- Everyone else knows how hard I try with you!
- You're always throwing him/her to the wolves.
- You can't even admit when your wrong.
- You've changed, I don't even recognize you anymore.
- It's your own fault, you keep taking him/her back?
- Its both of your faults for ruining your relationship.
- Well maybe if we had s*x more then I wouldn't hate you so much!
- I've lost all respect for you.
- You're the only person who has ever questioned me.
- If I didn't really want to be here and didn't love you, do you really think I would put up with your sh*t?
- I'm just playing.
- You need to calm down and stop overthinking.
- You just don't see it the way it is, your just weird.
- You always think that I'm doing something or out to get you.
- I do everything for you, how could you say I did this?
- It's your fault that I cheated!
- I never said that.
- You didn't see me do anything.
- You're just a very over-sensitive person.
- Nobody else sees him/her that way.
- You need to be stick up for me with this or we're done.

- You need to respect my privacy. I don't need to share EVERYTHING with you. (while he/she is demanding you share everything)
- He/she is a great father/mother. You're lucky to have him/her.
- Marriage takes hard work.
- It's not a big deal! Time to get over it!
- You're just paranoid.
- You're always complaining, just accept it and stop being a such a sourpuss.
- Even my ex wasn't as crazy as you.
- They love you. Your lucky to have them.
- I can't believe you would lie and say he/she does these things to you.
- You're the one with the terrible past so don't be so quick to judge others.
- Do you hear yourself?
- I have never yelled at you. I was just trying to be heard!
- You've been really distant lately.
- Your child can't be happy unless they do things my way!
- You don't really believe that do you?
- If you think I'm so bad, why don't you just leave?
- I wouldn't even call it abuse, you act like I do it all the while.
- I can have friends you know.
- You're the only one who doesn't see the truth.
- He/she takes care of you so you need to respect them!
- You're the one that wants to be like this! It's all coming from you.
- Something is really wrong with you, you should see a doctor.
- Why do you even exist, you should just die?
- I know you probably have someone to replace me, probably already have the next one lined up.

- You "two" need to stop this.
- You're just lucky that he/she puts up with you.
- You don't deserve him/her.
- You have an anger problem. You're the only one who acts like this.
- You don't remember anything right!
- He's under so much stress. It's not his fault, just leave him alone.
- I never asked you to do that, so why should I be thankful? I don't know why you're so upset.
- Well, that's your truth, not mine.
- I don't put you down that much... I could be much worse.
- Here you go playing the victim.
- You're not trying hard enough!
- You always want something... When will it be good enough for you?
- Nobody remembers any of those things.
- Obviously your medication isn't working, you need more!
- You're lucky that I'm even talking to you!
- My son/daughter did nothing wrong!
- You're over-reacting!
- You did this to our family.
- I only lied because I knew this is how you'd react.
- Do you want him to hit you? You're the one who pushed him to far!
- But you both look so good together.
- I don't believe he/she would ever do that!
- You're paranoid. I can't be with someone who doesn't trust me.
- You've made him/her so miserable. I've never seen them so depressed.
- You and your whole family are crazy!
- You always get things wrong, your terrible talking things out!

- You're just crazy and everyone agrees that you are!
- Why do you always scream and shout!
- You wouldn't really care if I committed suicide WOULD you?
- I'm sorry you feel that way.
- You should see the look on your face right now. Your acting insane!
- Look how good you have it with me.
- Stop being so entitled!
- You're just mad!
- You're putting words in my mouth.
- Is that really how you see me? That's really hurtful.
- We were playing around, remember? I didn't hurt you that bad, we were playing.
- That's in the past, get over it.
- He/she is sorry. Why can't you just forgive and forget! What you're doing is just keeping things up.
- Talk about that one more time and I'm going to lose it.
- You need to take responsibility and stop blaming everything on your parents!
- Where do you come up with this stuff! I'm not talking to you anymore!
- You need to get help.
- Do you think I got my family to lie for me?
- You're just stuck in the past!
- You're reading into this all wrong.
- You're imagining things.
- You just want a drama party and for people to pity you.
- I'm right, you're wrong, I don't ever want to hear you say that again!
- Are you sure you didn't hear wrong?
- He/she has done everything for you. What have you done in return, nothing?
- Someone must have hacked my account, it wasn't me!
- Well, you didn't stop it happening so you can't put ALL of the blame on me.

- I think you just need more sleep. You're not okay in the head.
- Nobody else will ever want someone like you.
- Why are you trying to hurt him/her?
- Maybe we should go see a counselor, then you'll see that it is you, not me.
- You're just a coward.
- You're like this with me because you're not happy.
- Nothing I ever do is good enough!
- You're just looking for drama! There's nothing to be upset about!
- Are you sure? Are you feeling okay? What is the matter with you?
- You never say what you did wrong.
- My friends always say how crazy you are, your embarrassing!
- I'm not getting involved in your "issues".
- But you're a match made in heaven.
- You don't appreciate him/her.
- Lots of people lie to the police/courts.
- But he/she makes really good money!
- You need to Man-up.
- You're always miserable!
- You would be nothing without me.
- Its all your fault!
- But you both always look so happy.
- But there always nice to me!
- You've ruined my night now.
- You'll never get anyone like me.
- Why do you do this to yourself?
- Their laying down the poison
- Their giving you the bullets to fire!
- Nobody else will believe you, I've already told them about you.

Reactive abuse.

Reactive abuse is when a victim reacts to a perpetrator's abuse. The victim may scream, swear, lash out physically or actually start to copy the behavior of the abuser. The abuser then tells the victim and others that they are, in fact, the abuser. Abusers rely on "reactive abuse" because it is their "proof" that the victim is actually the abuser, and not them. Abusers will keep bringing up these reactions in every argument. Reactive abuse is often used to justify going to the police or even filing for injunctions or non-molestation orders of their own. Reactive abuse is not the same as mutual abuse. Both partners can be equally abusive to one another and many survivors often ask themselves if they are abusive too, because of how they react. www.domesticshelters.org says that mutual abuse is very rare and many experts don't believe it exists. The power and control dynamics involved in domestic violence would make it nearly impossible for both partners to be abusive.

When domestic violence is present, there is always one who initiates or instigates the abuse in the relationship. Again it amounts to that one person needing the power and control over their victim. That's what abuse is – the imbalance of power. Don't believe anyone when they say, "Well, we were abusive to each other." Abusers will never accept responsibility for their actions and instead shift blame the abuse onto others. They often say their behavior is actually because of you being so needy or "a pain", that they are reacting to your abuse. Have you ever been told you owe them something, and to look at all they have done for you? Abusers know which buttons to push, they have been carefully monitoring you for a long time.

Abusers also have very short memories, denying their abuse to you and others, almost bewildered at the very thought of such bad behavior. It's you, you have anger issues, you have control issues and they are the poor helpless victims. You will find talking about your feelings very hard with abusers because they will accuse you of overreacting and making mountains out of molehills, trivializing you. It's a very difficult situation and often very hard to prove because of how covertly the perpetrators' abuse has been carried out.

Also trying to explain to an abuser that your reactions are because of their actions is impossible. You will find yourself explaining all the basic emotions and feelings that a 3-year-old should know. Even being 'nice' must be explained and they seem to simply have no concept of basic human interaction. Victims will think to themselves, 'if' I can just get them to understand why I'm so hurt, then they'll stop doing it. But they won't stop. They will pretend to be decent human beings, even showing complete understanding in front of others, but in reality, they would not have done these things in the first place if they were. Abusers will accuse the victim of feeling emotions they are intentionally provoking. It's normal to feel jealous if they are blatantly flirting with someone else, especially an ex! This is often over social media, using other supplies as backups and making themselves feel empowered. At what point does it become acceptable to ask to check their messages, or ask them to prove they are not doing something wrong?

It's highly likely the victim was once an exceptionally easy-going individual, intelligent with strong morals. But when someone uses these methods to intentionally provoke reactions, either in private or public to prove how 'hysterical' you are to others, it will turn the victim's outlook and moods upside down. Actively researching and taking time for healing after an encounter with an abuser is necessary.

It's important to remind the victim that it's common for them to be among the few who see the abusers' true colors. Abusers will surround themselves with a fan club of superficial friends.

1. Think of one of your close friends, what could you say to provoke a reaction?

2. What reaction do you think would be provoked?

3. Now, how could you get them to believe they have overreacted or taken you out of context.

The difference is choice, you choose not to provoke, to abuse.

EVEN GOOD PEOPLE HAVE THEIR LIMITS.

Projection & Triangulation

We all naturally use **projection**, it is human nature. For instance, if you're in a great mood, but your friend isn't. You continue to smile and maintain your positive mood, projecting it onto your friend. Or, another form of projection could be if your partner is in a bad mood, sees that you're smiling and happy, and they start yelling at you for being cheerful. Your partner is then projecting their mood onto you. Projection is a form of control and manipulation, gas-lighting is a common term used to describe someone who is being manipulated by psychological means into doubting their own sanity. Abusers simply can't allow others to be independent because it challenges them, makes life inconvenient, and uncomfortable, so they do everything they can to gain power and control over their victim. Often abusers will live in fantasy worlds where they refuse to see their own faults or acknowledge their failures, which means the blame that would usually be placed on them is projected onto their victims, preventing any type of learning. Abusers can and often are linked to psychopathic traits and narcissism. The same as psychopaths, abusers have little or no shame unless their image is at risk. They can and do goad by continuously criticizing, humiliating and degrading.

In projection, the victim's own opinions and feelings are picked away until their self image and self confidence are destroyed. Abusers can become easily bored so surround themselves with other people who are stimulating and praising them. Often they become quickly uninterested by anything that does not have a positive or thrilling result for them directly, using others as tools to 'get at' the victim. This 'triangulation' can make you feel confused, giving the impression that they are in high demand by their friends all the while. The purpose of this manipulation tactic is to create chaos and keep the victim off balance. Perpetrators using this technique will pit victims against each other for their approval. Flirting with others, inventing stories such as others are flirting with them or the victims friends don't really like them. At first they will seem exciting and all knowing, often making the victim feel quite inferior. Remember... Insecure people are easy to control.

They will accuse you of having anger and control issues. Often playing the victim to your friends and family when you react to their triangulation tactics. Abusers will blame you for all their woes, you never helped them, you're not supportive or you keep interfering in things. All this leads again to the victim accepting the abusive behaviour through fear, guilt or a lack of their own self worth – believing they 'deserve' the abuse.

Personal jokes are often used to attack the personality and character of the victim, again undermining confidence. This is often done as revenge for something they believe you have done to them. They will say you have no sense of humor or tell you to lighten up when you get offended. It is unfortunately also very possible that your abuser will destroy your things, especially personal items that mean a lot. They might crack or destroy your phone or 'lose' your bank card or car keys, then deny it. In long-term or severe cases of domestic abuse, the victims' identity can be destroyed and never recovered. They then need to begin the healing and rebuilding of who they are from the bottom up. It is very important at this point to include a good understanding of abuse, boundaries and the drug-like effect abuse can have to prevent another abusive relationship.

Triangulation in psychology is the name for a heartless form of manipulation in which one person seeks to punish or control someone via a third party. It often involves the use of threats of exclusion or strategies that aim to divide and conquer but also less subtle examples such as boasting about how much fun they had with there 'ex' last night. The third party does not necessarily need to be aware of the triangulation.

"Narcissists use triangulation to maintain control of family dynamics. The narcissist will pit siblings against each other in order to achieve their goals. The narcissist will lie to one child about the other in order to gain an accomplice in ganging up on their sibling. A narcissist will also lie to both children simultaneously, informing them that they are the favorite child."

Quote: Tina Fuller, Narcissistic Parents

"Toxic people have an incredible ability to triangulate third parties into abusing a victim. This is done on purpose so the toxic person's hands 'stay clean' from the abuse."

Quote: Shannon Thomas, southlakecounseling.org

"Narcissists bring a third person into the mix, many times without that other person knowing. It's also called 'abuse by proxy". Sometimes, the narcissists will even have that third person contact us and 'pass along a message' just to see our reaction. Narcissists want to use another person to abuse us so they can claim innocence. Triangulation is just a way for narcissists to maintain power and control over there targets."

Quote: @FreedomFromNarcissisticAndEmotionalAbuse

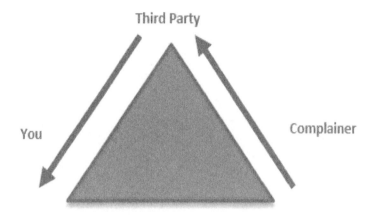

Image: bates-communications.com

Emotional isolation and neglect

'Dehumanizing' is often used by abusers to demand respect. Everything and anything you do wrong, no matter how slight will not go unpunished. You are expected to defer to them on everything, but it's only one-way! If you do try to communicate you are shut down, the subject changed or plain ignored. The victim goes from being showered with non-stop attention and admiration to suddenly feeling isolated and neglected. The abuser seems to have become 'bored' by them. This is when the abuser shows their normal self, the mask slips away and they will become very annoyed that the victim is interested in continuing the passionate relationship that they created in the first place, it's hard work for them. Abusers will manipulate you, or the situation to stop you from socialising, creating drama, distraction or begging you not to go out. They are very good at making the victim believe it's their choice not to go see friends or even not be allowed to leave the house without the abuser. Abusers often cause an argument preventing the victim from even wanting to go out. They may have told family or friends that you don't want to see them, or make excuses why you cannot see them.

Often abusers are telling you one story, others something else. They'll tell co-workers, friends, and the victim's family that they are unstable, argumentative, needy, and abusive. When these misinformed or 'enablers' say something, the victim often chooses to 'keep the peace by not setting the record straight. This becomes the norm and isolation follows. Withholding affection is again very common, they won't touch you or refuse sexual relations and 'closeness' out of spite, to punish you or get you to do something. Victims often feel more alone when with an abuser, unable to communicate out of a fear of their reaction. One massive red flag, one which you should never ignore is indifference. When you're hurt or crying, they do nothing. For example, if you come in after hurting your back and end up collapsing on the floor in pain, crying out, and unable to move. The response you will often get from abusers is "you are an inconvenience", hindrance, or needy. Remember, if it's in front of one of there/your friends or family, the 'act' of the loving caring partner will switch on.

Ivory Tower Syndrome

ivory tower noun

Definition of *ivory tower*

1   : an impractical often escapist attitude marked by aloof lack of concern with or interest in practical matters or urgent problems

2   : a secluded place that affords the means of treating practical issues with an impractical often escapist attitude

Credit: merriam-webster.com

Abusers will try to force the victim's image of them, to see the abuser as the centre of the victim's world, almost like an attention seeking child. Interrupting whatever you're doing

because they are more important and disputing your feelings. If you're on the phone or texting, they might get in your face and will make it very clear that the attention should be on them, not anyone else. Whatever the victim feels, they will say it's wrong for feeling like that, or that's not how you're actually feeling and they will then try to gaslight you into believing you're actually feeling something else. If you're ill, they will always be worse! If it's your birthday, they will ruin it. Whatever the occasion, be wary of them ruining it and playing the victim or crying wolf to gain the attention they need.

Often how they treat the victims will lead to a discussion about their abusive past, how they are depressed or the trauma they have suffered from a crazy ex (abusers have a lot of crazy ex's). This is often an attempt at making you feel sorry for them, changing the subject and refocusing the discussion. They will attempt to force a bond over their complex emotional state and give you the urge to help or 'fix' them for the better.

Be warned, abusers rarely change, they will cry wolf, sometimes apologize but in the end, they are the wolf! A pattern will soon emerge, apologising will only happen in order for them to gain the upper hand. In fact, often they will bring this up in further arguments and blame the victim for their actions.

Do you know anyone like this?

Codependency

A **codependent relationship** is when something you do is in reaction to your abuser's behavior (not to be mistaken with reactive abuse). More commonly associated with drug use and alcoholism, codependency in relationships is when the drug is replaced by the abuser. They need you to boost their own self-esteem and you may have forgotten how to live any other way. It's a vicious circle of unhealthy behavior and imbalance.

You might be codependent if you:

- are unhappy in the relationship, but fear alternatives.
- consistently neglect your own needs for the sake of theirs.
- Have a desperate need to please others.
- ditch friends and sideline your family to please your partner.
- frequently seek out your partner's approval.
- criticize yourself through your abuser's eyes.
- ignoring your own instincts.
- make a lot of sacrifices to please the other person, but it's not reciprocated.
- would rather live in the current state of chaos than be alone.
- Have Blurry boundaries.

- bite your tongue and repress your feelings to keep the peace.
- feel responsible and take the blame for something they did.
- defend your abuser when others point out what's happening.
- try to "rescue" them from themselves.
- Have a need to control.
- Have a fear of rejection.
- feel guilty when you stand up for yourself.
- think you deserve this treatment.
- believe that nobody else could ever want to be with you.
- change your behavior in response to guilt; your abuser.
- says, "I can't live without you," so you stay.
- Have an inability to form loving relationships.

There is also a massive selfishness and a thirst for attention from the abuser. Abusers will drain the energy from you, consuming your entire life leaving you exhausted and confused. You will start to seek answers elsewhere, health, fitness, even blaming others for how you feel. At first, you would have been drawn in by the thought that you could fix them or you were the only one who could make them happy. However remember, the truth is: no one can fill the black void of a true abuser's soul! Abusers have so much in common with dark personality disorders, often themselves being hidden psychopaths and narcissists. When the problem is this deep, there is no helping them and you will be left drained and broken while they move onto someone who is unaware of their dark side.

No contact is the only real safe route to take.

Lying and Excuses

Abusers are very good at manipulation as we have already discussed. They will use any method they can including lying to get the results they want. If that lie is found out, they simply ignore that they have been caught and move on to the next falsehood. They will constantly blame others and spend more time rationalising their behaviour than trying to resolve any conflict. This includes focusing on the mistakes the victim has made, not on their own mistakes in order to throw off the argument. Victims can become confused at the lies being told, often because there is simply not a need for that lie to be told! It's almost as if they want the victim to find them out, craving the drama that is caused. Again, this is where you might be drawn into the circular arguments, explaining the simple values and boundaries of human nature to someone who can be described in no other way, but a brick wall. One red flag to be aware of, is an unusual amount of 'crazy' exes. Anyone who did not come back grovelling on their hands and knees may have been labelled jealous, bipolar, mad or any number of derogatory names. When they do come back, they are held on standby to make the victim jealous or to hook up with if the opportunity presents itself. Make no mistake, the abuser will speak about their current victim in the same way after the discard phase!

Coercive Control

Coercive control – Abusive power and control

From Wikipedia, the free encyclopedia

WIKIPEDIA
The Free Encyclopedia

Abusive power and control (also **controlling behavior** and **coercive control**) is commonly used by an abusive person to gain and maintain power and control over another person in order to subject that victim to psychological, physical, sexual, or financial abuse. The motivations of the abuser are varied and can include devaluation, envy, personal gain, personal gratification, psychological projection, or just for the sake of the enjoyment of exercising power and control.[1]

Controlling abusers use tactics to exert power and control over their victims. The tactics themselves are psychologically and sometimes physically abusive. Control may be exerted through economic abuse, limiting the victim, as they may not have the means to resist or leave the abuse.[2] The goal of the abuser is to control, intimidate, and influence the victim to feel they do not have an equal voice in the relationship.[3]

Manipulators and abusers often control their victims with a range of tactics, including, but not limited to, positive reinforcement (such as praise, superficial charm, flattery, ingratiation, love bombing, smiling, gifts, attention), negative reinforcement (taking away aversive tasks or items), intermittent or partial reinforcement, psychological punishment (such as nagging, silent treatment, swearing, threats, intimidation, emotional blackmail, guilt trips, inattention) and traumatic tactics (such as verbal abuse or explosive anger).[4]

The vulnerabilities of the victim are exploited with those who are particularly vulnerable being most often selected as targets.[4][5][6] Traumatic bonding (also popularly known as Stockholm syndrome) can occur between the abuser and victim as the result of ongoing cycles of abuse in which the intermittent reinforcement of reward and punishment creates powerful emotional bonds that are resistant to change and a climate of fear.[7] An attempt may be made to normalise, legitimise, rationalise, deny, or minimise the abusive behaviour, or blame the victim for it.[8][9][10]

Isolation, gaslighting, mind games, lying, disinformation, propaganda, destabilisation, brainwashing, and divide and rule are other strategies that are often used. The victim may be plied with alcohol or drugs or deprived of sleep to help disorientate them.[11][12] Based on statistical evidence, certain personality disorders correlate with abusive tendencies of individuals with those specific personality disorders when also compiled with abusive childhoods themselves. [13]

The seriousness of coercive control in modern Western societies has been increasingly realised with changes to the law in several countries so it is a definable criminal offence. In conjunction with this there have been increased attempts by the legal establishment to understand the characteristics and effects of coercive control in legal terminology. For example, on January 1, 2019, Ireland enacted the Domestic Violence Act 2018, which allowed for the practice of coercive control to be identifiable based upon its effects on the victim. And on this basis defining it as: 'any evidence of deterioration in the physical, psychological, or emotional welfare of the applicant or a dependent person which is caused directly by fear of the behaviour of the respondent'.[14] On a similar basis of attempting to understand and stop the widespread practice of coercive control, in 2019, the UK government made teaching about what coercive control was a mandatory part of the education syllabus on relationships.[15] While coercive control is often considered in the context of an existing intimate relationship, when it is used to elicit a sexual encounter it is legally considered as being a constituent part of sexual abuse or rape. When it is used to begin and maintain a longer term intimate relationship it is considered to be a constituent element of sexual slavery.

Coercive control is when an abuser repeatedly does something in a way that makes their victim feel isolated, controlled, dependent, or scared. Often saying they'll harm the victim, themselves, pets, or family members.

These types of behavior are common examples of coercive control as well as using both physical and emotional abuse as described earlier, this list is by no means exhaustive, how many have happened to you?

- Isolating the victim from friends and family.

- Controlling someone's money.

- Monitoring a person's movements and activities.

- Repeatedly putting someone down, calling them names, or telling them they're worthless.

- Threatening to harm someone or their children or pets.

- Threatening to publish private information about someone.

- Falsely reporting someone to the police.

- Damaging goods or property.

- Forcing someone to take part in criminal activity or child abuse.

- Gaslighting.

- Reinforcing the roles within a relationship.

- Manipulating others (flying monkeys) or engaging in parental alienation.

- Controlling what you wear, how you look, how often you wash and what essentials you can use.

- Sexual coercion, using sex to control you or get what they want.

Some of these behaviors can also be other offenses as well as coercive control. So a perpetrator can be arrested for more than one offense, for the same behavior. For example, if a perpetrator broke a phone as part of their coercive control then they could be arrested and charged for coercive control and also the offense of criminal damage. An abuser damages the victim's possessions but rarely their own property or the property of others in the household, again showing a deliberate action and not of a loss of self-control. An abuser will only be guilty of the offense of coercive control if their behavior has had a serious effect on the person and that he/she knew or ought to have known that their behavior would have a serious effect on that person. It is also very common for abusers to use those you love to further control you, often children or pets. Abusers can threaten to harm, kidnap, or even claim they will 'take the children from them'. Abusers will also use guilt, saying the victim is breaking up the family. Remembering that Children do have a voice is very important and speaking with them away from any influencing party is routinely practiced by professionals to gain a more accurate and 'bigger picture.

Social Abuse

Social abuse is humiliation, this cruel treatment includes public threats, intimidation, and gossip. As well as joking at your expense, constant heckling or teasing to provoke a response to then project the blame onto you. It also includes tickling, touching, kissing, or other forms of physical acts that you have asked your partner to refrain from in public – this is entirely dependent on your, your feelings, and what you have asked them not to do. Any behavior designed to upset you in front of others is social abuse.

Some examples of Social Abuse;

- Refuses to socialize with your family or friends.

- Encourages friends who are abusive.

- Demands you move away from friends and a supportive environment.

- Monitors your social activities.

- Alienates you from your family and friends.

- Treats you disrespectfully in front of others.

- Tells secrets or embarrassing stories about you.

- Refuses to let you work outside the home.

- Demands that you account for all your time with social contacts.

- Controls who you can visit and when.

- Gossips or spread rumors about you.

It's expected that most of the above are practiced by an abuser as part of the abusive relationship.

The disclosure of confidential information or embarrassing events to co-workers and friends is also classed as socially abusive behaviour. Gossiping, spreading rumors, and playing mind games or gaslighting are effective means of controlling others.

So is using social media. Abusers can be masters at tearing up and looking 'ever-so-sincere' before disclosing embarrassing information about their victim in the form of "sharing concerns" and "advice". The only true-fire way of fighting these games is not to play. Do not waste your time outwitting the abuser, every time you clear up one issue, another two have popped up. Going no contact is the hardest thing in the world (especially if you care for them still, which is often the case in abusive relationships due to the trauma bonding effect). It is the most rewarding and only truly safe path to take with abusers. It is also very common that when a victim leaves an abusive relationship and the abuser can no longer control them directly, they will try and control how others see them. The misinformation will feel unfair and often leads to professionals getting involved such as police, social services, and other safeguarding parties especially if there are children involved. Staying above it, and trusting that eventually others will see the truth is the only way to avoid the mental damage this abuse can do.

By distancing yourself, going '**_grey rock_**' or '**_yellow rock_**' the survivor is able to maintain some sense of self and prevents them from falling into the trap the abuser sets for them, namely, provoking them in front of others to make them appear guilty.

No Contact (No Rock)   Gray Rock*   Yellow Rock*

Gray Rock examples;

(1) Not leaving yourself open, communicating in writing (text, email) so there is a paper trail, and lies are easier to document. There are Co-parenting apps that difficult to falsify: OurFamilyWizard, AppClose, TalkingParents. Others are available.
(2) Short answers about logistics only.
(3) Not showing anger, defending, or explaining because any time you show emotion, they turn it against you.
(4) Using 'professional' mannerisms such as, "You opinion is noted. I have a different view." And not one word more.

Yellow Rock is like Gray Rock, except you include "Thank you," "Please," and "Hello" in your communication.

- *The phrase "Gray Rock" [Grey Rock] was coined in the article: "The Gray Rock Method of Dealing With Psychopaths" 180Rule.com. Yellow Rock was coined by Tina Swithin, OneMomsBattle.com*

I also want to bring attention to the 'privilege' in this section, where the perpetrator defines their role in the relationship (Ivory Tower). For instance, the traditional definition of male and female roles, the female must not question her man's needs, desires or actions. Believing they are above common people, paying others to do jobs that are beneath them, standing over them feeling Superior.

Abusers will often dominate and make all the important decisions, directly or through manipulation of the victim.

Sexual Abuse

Sexual abuse, is abusive sexual behaviour by one person upon another. This includes rape and sexual assault. This type of abuse can have ongoing physical and emotional effects. Professional counselling is often needed.

Victims can be reluctant to discuss or report sexual abuse. The British Crime Survey indicates that in cases of serious sexual assault, the rapist is actually more likely to be a current or ex-partner, or known to the victim (89% of female and 83% of male victims), with only a minority of rapes being committed by strangers. Sexual abuse can include the use of force, threats, manipulation, drugs, sleeping or intimidation. These are often used to make another person perform sexual acts or coerce them into having sex when they do not want to. It may include forcing the victim to use pornography or have sex with other people.

Sexual abuse also includes behaviour which degrades a person's sexuality. The 'home office 2001a' report found that 53% of homophobic abuse reported to the police happens in the home in contrast to 17% on the street.

If you suspect anyone of sexual abuse, please report it to the police. Sarah's law is a method for you to check your partner for offenses relating to child sexual abuse if you suspect anything. Any offenses disclosed during a request for Sarah's law will be dealt with in the same way as reporting a crime directly to the police.

All rape and sexual assaults are serious but the terms rape and 'sexual assault' are used simply to differentiate between two types of offense.

- Rape is when a male intentionally penetrates a vagina, anus, or mouth with a penis, without the other person's consent.

- Assault by penetration is when a person penetrates another person's vagina or anus with any part of the body other than a penis, or by using an object, without the person's consent.

The definition overall of 'sexual' or 'indecent' assault is simply an act of physical, psychological and emotional violation in the form of a sexual act, inflicted on someone without their consent. Not all cases of sexual assault involve violence, cause physical injury or leave visible marks. Sexual assault can cause severe distress, emotional harm and injuries which can't be seen – all of which can take a long time to recover from.

The following are examples of sexual abuse:

- Insisting on anything sexual that frightens or hurts you.

- Withholding sex as a form of control.

- Demanding sex/Forcing sex.

- Name-calling with sexual epithets.

- Demanding sex after a violent incident.

- Alleging that you have a history of prostitution on legal papers.

- Forcing you to engage in prostitution or pornography.

- Forcing you to have sex with others besides your partner.

- Unwanted touching.

- Refusing to use safe sex practices.

- Controlling your decisions about pregnancy and/or abortion.

- Videotaping or photographing sexual acts and posting the footage without your permission.

- Preventing you from using birth control.

Financial/Economic Abuse

Economic or financial abuse can start subtle and is often very hard to detect, often financial abuse is intended to make it financially impossible for the victim to leave or have a life outside of the relationship. Abusers have a lack of understanding or lack of regard for others' boundaries and rights to their own money. Often they will take or misuse someone else's money or belongings for their own gain.

An example is;

A man's brother is mentally challenged and has his benefits going into a post office account. His brother and sister who jointly care for him, seeing the amount of money in this account believe they have a right to this money simply because the mentally incapable brother does not have the capacity to understand the value of money and does not 'need' that amount. This results in the capable siblings stealing money from his account in order to buy a new car or holidays.

Financial abuse can be anything to do with money, property, or belongings. It can often be pushed under the carpet and forgotten just to keep the peace. The effects of such abuse on the victim can be very harmful and not just deprive the victim but disadvantage them in areas, further leading to the thoughts they are incapable of looking after themselves. It's important to remember that financial abuse doesn't always involve a crime like theft or fraud. Examples of financial abuse;

- Borrowing money and/or not giving it back.

- Stealing the victim's belongings.

- Taking the victims wages, pension, or other types of income.

- Taking or asking for money as payment for normal things couples or friends do, such as visiting or spending time together.

- Removing money from bank accounts which do not belong to you, or joint accounts without telling the other person.

- Forcing or manipulating the victim to sell their home.

- Stealing or holding bank cards, details, etc.

- Forcing or manipulating changes in wills, property, or inheritance.

- Unexplained money loss which cannot be explained and is being stolen by the abuser, creating situations so complex you cannot get to grips with everything.

- No money to pay for essentials such as rent, bills, and food, often having to ask or beg for essentials.

- Refused access to check their own bank accounts or balance.

- Changes in the standards of living i.e. not having items or things they would usually have or need such as grooming items or clothing.

- Unusual or inappropriate purchases in bank statements.

- Using inappropriate powers such as the power of attorney to access another person's money without their consent.

- Consistently standing back and letting the other person pay for everything.

- Saying you will pay half towards the bills, then making excuses and never paying.

Again this list is not inclusive of every type of financial abuse. Financial abuse can be committed by anyone anywhere, even people employed to provide care. Spouses, friends, family, and neighbours are all capable as well as volunteers, even strangers. Financial abuse can affect anyone but often takes place where there is an unequal balance of power. These are often victims of another form of abuse such as domestic abuse or violence, individuals with learning disabilities or medical conditions where strong medication is needed are especially vulnerable.

Dating Abuse & Red Flags

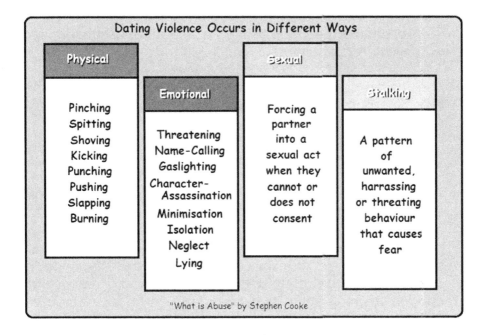

Dating Violence Occurs in Different Ways

Physical
Pinching
Spitting
Shoving
Kicking
Punching
Pushing
Slapping
Burning

Emotional
Threatening
Name-Calling
Gaslighting
Character-Assassination
Minimisation
Isolation
Neglect
Lying

Sexual
Forcing a partner into a sexual act when they cannot or does not consent

Stalking
A pattern of unwanted, harrassing or threating behaviour that causes fear

"What is Abuse" by Stephen Cooke

Dating abuse is the term given to abuse while two partners are intimately dating, more often to those under the age of 25. Surveys conducted by the NSPCC and End Violence Against Women campaign show that approximately 40% of young people experience abuse in their teens. The surveys also point out that sexual violence is higher in young people than any other age range with 1-in-5 teenage girls being assaulted at the hands of their boyfriend.

Additional studies have also shown that young people who are subject to abuse are at a higher risk of further violence, riskier sexual behaviour, substance abuse and eating disorders than people who have known healthy relationships.

The differences between healthy and toxic relationships.

Reading and familiarizing yourself with this book will help you recognize the signs of both a healthy relationship and an unhealthy relationship.

The differences between them can be obvious from an outsider, but get very muddled when you experience things yourself.

Characteristics of a Healthy relationship.

Good communication is at the heart of a healthy relationship. Both simple and difficult subjects need to be discussed and problems do arise which need to be talked about and a decision made together. Trust, respect and honesty are signs of a healthy relationship. Could you trust your partner around someone else who liked them, or respect them enough to allow their own boundaries and separate friends? Please see our book "Be Abuse Aware - Boundaries").

It's also important that you enjoy spending time together, and equally enjoy spending time with your own family and friends apart from each other. Seeing both partners as equals and openly discussing relationship problems and sexual choices will allow for a better future.

Behaviors that might indicate abuse.

Some general red flags to watch for are past patterns of abuse, cruelty to animals or children, and hypersensitivity. Abusers can be easily angered and they react aggressively and blow things out of proportion very quickly. They tend to blame everyone but themselves. They often feel someone is out to get them, holding them back, or is not supporting them how they should.

Examples of Verbal and emotional abuse:

- Name-calling, saying things to others about you, and saying things that make you feel guilty.
- 'Raging'. Temper tantrums are often used and yelling, screaming, or threatening to hurt themselves or those you care about.
- Pretending to be concerned about you when really it is control – "don't take that job it's too hard", "don't drive there, it's too dark" etc. – abusers will often start making all their partners decisions from what there wearing, to who they talk to,
- Putting you down, you look fat, that dress is horrible or what you say or do is always wrong,
- Jealousy, often mistaken for love is the opposite of trust and accusations of flirting, cheating, or being consistently suspicious,
- Embarrassing you in public or causing a scene in front of others,
- Threatening to end the relationship or moving too quickly in order to trap you,
- Spreading rumors and lies about you to your friends, family, or other people,
- Blaming you for the abuse or denying that it is happening.

Examples of physical abuse:

- Any action that physically hurts another's body,
- Shoving, Pinching, Scratching, Slapping, Spitting,
- Pushing, Punching, Hitting, Kicking, Hair pulling,
- Strangulation (also during sex, is now classed as abuse under the 2021 Domestic Abuse Act – UK –) or other life-threatening abuse.

Examples of Sexual abuse:

- Unwanted harassment, touching, and kissing,
- Forcing you to have sex or perform other sexual acts,
- Manipulating or forcing you to engage in sex acts with others or animals,
- Not allowing you to use birth control or protection.

If you start dating, it's a good idea to give it at least 3-6 months before committing yourself to a relationship. That doesn't mean seeing other people or treating them as an option but keep on your guard, look out for the mask slipping and get to know them before falling head over heels in love.

Red Flags are behaviours which point to them being abusive in the future. It's never easy to spot the red flags of an abusive relationship early on. In fact, many abusers seem absolutely perfect on the surface. In the early stages of a relationship the dream partner, promising the earth, utter and complete happiness. The below is a bullet style list of red flags to watch out for.

How many can you relate too?

- They want to rush into a new relationship too quickly.

- Alcohol or substance abuse, they need help and support – not by you, by professionals and it's not your job or fault by protecting yourself and your family.

- Embarrassing you or putting you down in private or in front of others.

- They're rude to strangers or people in the service industry.

- Looking at you or acting in ways that scare you.

- Jealousy! A big one we can all have, but how we manage it matters. This can lead to obsession and controlling behaviour. Things such as constantly looking at your partners phone, demanding to read what you put to others on text's, social media and not allowing you to be alone with others are early signs of jealousy.

- That 'GUT' feeling, our brains have been trained from birth to override our natural feelings so in dating and meeting new friends, always trust your gut – its not restricted by all that learning you have done.

- They never initiate constantly relying on you to speak, arrange dates or initiate intimacy.

- All their exes are 'crazy' or abusive.

- Controlling behavior such as who you see, where you go, or what you do (often under the pretense of it's for your own good, or I'm just caring about you).

- Their emotion's make you feel unsafe, they get angry or express themselves aggressively.

- Keeping you away from friends or family, reducing your ability to confide in others for support (your support network).

- They do not take any notice of your physical and emotional boundaries, often pushing them in 'innocent' ways.

- Lying about small or big things.

- Their hot and cold towards you, possibly as part of a controlling 'plan'.

- Taking control of your money or refusing to give you money for things you need (always keep your finances separate from others – greed is the route to all evil and no-one else's business!).

- Love-Bombing, gone are the days of the old gentleman and now we have to be alert for this fake form of showing affection early on. The simple difference between love bombing and being old school; old school lasts forever and love bombing leads into the cycle of abuse

- Not listening to you, interrupting and not allowing you to have your say on something.

- Making decisions for you, such as what to wear or what you will eat! Not allowing you to make your own decisions and passing it off as a joke.

- Scared to have that 'relationship talk', its hard and the fear of rejection can weigh heavily but its necessary and avoiding or refusing to talk about it is a red flag.

- Saying 'it was only a joke' when they do something bad or hurt your feelings.

- Telling you that your parenting is bad and threatening to harm or take away your children.

- Constantly needing reassurance, we're all insecure but it's not healthy to rely solely on other peoples validation. They need to work on themselves before jumping back into the dating pool.

- They do not split the bill, refuse to pay or expect you to pay.

- Not allowing you to work or attend school.

- Your friends get 'bad' vibes or don't want to spend any time with them.

- Blaming you for their abuse (projecting), or acting like it's not happening at all (Gaslighting).

- They spend more time hitting on the bartender than you!

- They know too much about you, things you have not told them.

- Lack of communication, keeping some things to yourself is normal and healthy but just assuming you should know things and getting upset when you don't is a red flag.

- Twist's reality, making you doubt your own perceptions and saying things like "I never did that" or "You're too sensitive".

- Destroying or damaging your property, saying things like "look what you made me do" or saying "it's your fault I did that".

- Having opinions about everything you say and do!

- You seem to be used to make someone else jealous.

- Setting rules, often like certain clothing, appearance, who you can 'hang out' with, how often you can use social media or asking you to delete your accounts and who can be your 'friends'.

- Putting you down, your weight, dress sense, intelligence to low or too high (you're too smart for your own good), self esteem is too high (You think too much of yourself), your ugly, you'd be pretty if... etc.

- Threatening to hurt you, your friends/family or your pets.

- Using you for lifts, babysitting or what you can do for them.

- They spend more time texting their friend on your date.

- Talking about marriage early on.

- Excessive sarcasm or using humor in a mean way by regularly pointing out your flaws (There's a difference between roasting each other in a fun, consensual way and jokes that make you feel bad about yourself).

- Racist views, behavior or comments.

- They bring a friend to your date.

- Intimidating you with weapons guns, knives or fists (clenching them when they disagree) or are 'fed up' of something or someone.

- Assaulting you, such as shoving, slapping, choking, spitting or hitting you.

- How do they react when you want time away from them? Responding poorly when you need space often means they are very possessive and have trouble meeting their own emotional needs.

- Extreme emotional reactions to events are a sign of an unstable personality.

- Attempting to stop you from pressing charges.

- They don't ask you any questions.

- Sexist views, behaviors or comments.

- Threatening to commit suicide because of something you've done or threatening to do (like leaving them because of there behaviour).

- Threatening to kill you or those close to you.

- They start to, or want to rely on you as their sole support for serious mental health issues or past traumas.

- Saying others are 'below them'.

GRANDIOSE DELUSIONS

- Taking the mick out of others, strangers, friends or family!

- They check in to frequently – checking up and communicating at the right times and frequency is an early green flag (a good thing) but excessively is unhealthy and a red flag! Do they check up on you when they know your out with friends? Giving each other space is healthy.

- Having bad relationships with friends and family.

- More than an hour late for your date, and constantly telling you their 5 mins away.

- Smothering you, like telling you to quit your job as they will take care of you, constant contact etc.

- Early signs that everything is about them, their needs, expectations and how they want things to be.

- Borrowing money all the while. Saying things like "You know I'm good for it" and not paying it back, or paying it back in different small amounts, making it difficult to keep track if they have paid you back at all!

- Pressuring you to have sex when you don't want to, or do other sexual things you're not comfortable with or simply do not want to do. This includes carrying on at you after saying 'No' until you give in to keep the peace!

- Angry outbursts – going from 0-60 very quickly over small things.

- Homophobic or transphobic views or comments.

- They do not take responsibility, blaming everything on others.

- You mention something your ex did which was either abusive or made you feel terrible and they take their side.

- They are not motivated, give up easy, complain a lot! Not a massive red flag but still something to be aware of.

- Pressuring you to use drugs or alcohol.

- They are at a very different life stage, such as wanting to sell up and travel the world when you want to settle down!

- Hiding things early on, like a wedding ring or another relationship.

- Prevent you from using birth control, threatening you not to or pressuring you to become pregnant before you're ready.

- They always want you to prioritize them over your own family, friends or children!

- They don't have many friends – they may be loners or by keeping their friendship circle small they avoid drama but constantly having new friends or friends that are only friends because they are 'incentivised' somehow.

- The sadness type – close when your sad, but they are not happy when your happy and successful.

- The 'group' junkie – nice to you one-on-one but in a group constantly put you down.

- There only your friend/partner until you question them or say no - then all hell brakes lose and your punished.

- How they treat their enemies is a very good indication of character – remember, you could be the enemy some day!

- The good vibes only... that is fine for yourself but applying it to others who maybe down, cutting them off if they need to talk about something and saying 'good vibes only' is a red flag.

- You realise your more 'yourself' with them not being around.

- Being dismissive of your interests and achievements and changing the subject to what they have done or how good their family is.

- Constantly telling others bad things or lies about you. Gossiping about others is a good chance their going to gossip about you too. This often includes screenshots.

- Always asking for favors but never returning them.

- When you cannot trust anything they say – actions speak louder than words.

- When you get a message from them, you get nervous or anxious.

- They only pay you attention when there's no-one else.

- It's always last minute cancellation of plans.

- Being able to apologize or say they did something wrong.

- Constantly asking for advice, but never talking it and involving you in there drama.

- Constantly wanting to say something to them, but having to hold your tongue.

Risk Factors of Domestic Abuse

There are numerous risk factors that can increase the intensity and frequency of domestic abuse.

Identifying abuse is only the first step, it's now time to get your support network in place. The following is a list of perpetual triggers that increase domestic abuse.

Alcohol misuse. Alcohol consumption itself doesn't cause domestic abuse, but when it is used by an abuser, it will increase the severity and frequency. If the victim is also misusing alcohol, this can increase their susceptibility to abuse.

Age. Younger people are more at risk of abuse simply due to their inexperience than older people. (Walby & Allen 2004).

Ending the relationship. Victims are more at risk of serious abuse after leaving the relationship. Abusers will attempt to use more extreme methods of regaining control and are known to falsely report victims to authorities in order to punish them. Gender.

Gender plays a crucial role in violence and abuse in society. Both males and females can be victims and perpetrators of abuse. Research has shown that the rates of abuse differ significantly between men and women (Stanko 2006, p. 552). This report shows women are significantly more at risk of domestic abuse than men.

Pregnancy. There is a common belief that having a child can bring a couple closer together. This is not true and evidence has suggested that abuse can often start during pregnancy (30% of DV starts during pregnancy – British Medical Association 1998).

A victims 'cycle of abusive partners'. Often victims are so used to being controlled and in a world full of drama they will seek out a similar partner in the future to fill this 'void' they perceive in themselves. Often this will lead to avoiding real nurturing relationships or 'good' partners because they find them boring. This cycle is often associated with drug dependency for an example of how the victim can feel about future partners and their need for this type of partner. Remaining single in order to heal is so important here because the victim needs to re-adjust their boundaries and self-confidence so they can be happy in a future relationship. This should not be confused with the Cycle of abuse/Violence theory developed by Lenore Walker in 1979, The battered woman. This theory is used to explain the cycle of abuse within a single relationship only.

Illness and Unemployment. Illness and unemployment will add to the stress of a person, building on the 'tension-building' stage of abuse. Often this coincides with financial or legal issues. Illness can also be seen by an abuser as another form of control over their victim. Playing on another's vulnerability to subjugate their self-esteem and confidence further.

RISK FACTORS

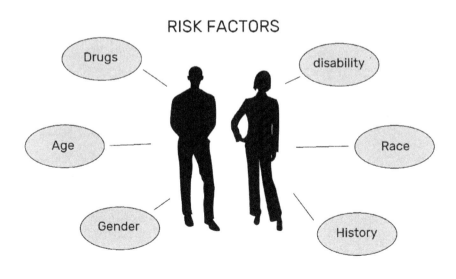

Parental Alienation

Parental alienation is complex and there is no single definition. CAFCASS recognizes parental alienation as "when a child's resistance or hostility towards one parent is not justified and is the result of psychological manipulation by the other parent."

With this type of abuse, it's important that all other risk factors such as domestic abuse are resolved first to allow for children to be safe. Children can reject the other parent or resist spending time with them because of the alienating behaviors of the other parent. This type of abuse does have a varying impact on individual children depending on the child's resilience and vulnerability. Alienation can occur quite openly such as a parent constantly badmouthing the other parent, physically stopping contact, forbidding discussion about them, and creating the impression in the child's mind that the other parent dislikes or does not love the child.

Tactics used can also be quite insidious such as talking about their experiences as a child and saying you (the child) are too young to understand what your own eyes are telling you and will understand as you get older, this is also gaslighting and a dangerous manipulation technique.

Isolating children from their support network, terrorizing them, and denying them their emotional needs. Parents who alienate create a false belief that the other parent is dangerous or unworthy, often portraying the picture that they are perfect, their life is so much better than the main carer.

Limited examples;

- Talking about their own experiences or third party lives to influence your relationships with either parent.

- Taking over the conversations when trying to talk about something that happened so they don't have to admit responsibility and 'look bad'.

- Attempting to manipulate the situation using gaslighting or other methods to see things from their point of view.

- Saying that the 'details' are not important when they are explaining their version of the truth.

- Justifying the actions of themselves or another that has been witnessed by putting the blame onto someone else, normally the alienated parent.

- Lies or says a half-truth so that you start to question the other parent.

- Using phrases such as 'I'm going, to be honest, you are old enough now, do you know what your …. did?"

- Saying how the alienated parent hurt them, caused them pain, and damaged them so you sympathize with their side.

- Showering the child with gifts and saying the other parent doesn't care enough to do this, or criticizes the other parent saying they don't treat them.

- Saying things like "there is no bad blood between us" or "we will always put you, children, first" then proceeding to say the other parent is a liar.

- Saying they miss and love the children and hate not seeing them more making out the other parent is stopping them from seeing the children.

- Making jokes between comments about the other parent to curtail the conversation away from what they have just said and preventing confronting or denying the 'said' comments.

- Saying they love you more than the other parent.

- Not accepting responsibility even when they know what they have done.

- Saying they will do things but with no intention of actually carrying these out, making excuses why these have not been carried out and often using the situation to make the children feel sorry for them.

Remember that phrase "in the child's best interests."

The effect of alienation on children can be lifelong. Their sense of identity, self-esteem, and confidence as well as their morals and beliefs can all be negatively affected by such actions. Post-separation, regularly assessing your own behaviour and the best interests of the child is very important, especially if there are strong negative emotions to the other parent.

Health and well-being

The impacts of domestic abuse on anyone cannot be understated, leading to depression, anxiety, aggression, trauma-related symptoms, self-harm, eating disorders, substance abuse, and C-PTSD. The effects are diverse, long-lasting, and debilitating, including detriments to physical and mental health, increased rates of suicide and self-harm, increased alcohol and drug misuse, as well as rises in the likelihood of being unemployed and becoming homeless. In most cases, the basis of abuse lies in sociology-cultural norms such as dowry, child marriage, a need for control, personality disorders, and normalization or inherited views of violence against women. Any form of abuse can cause or lead to serious physical and psychological effects. In my own personal experience of abuse, because of my old school values and 'sticking' it out for 25 years, my memory and concentration was massively affected, even now I still suffer 'mind drops' where I return to this state of numbness and memory loss which affects my daily living. Victims of domestic violence do suffer many mixed emotions such as fear, confusion, anger, numbness, guilt, and shame. Many victims do try to cover up the visible effects of violence with makeup or covering the bruises or scratches with clothes. Getting help for abuse in a timely manner can help prevent the long-term impact of abuse on your mental health. If you believe you are suffering from abuse, and start noticing your memory is suffering, you have word-finding difficulty, or are forgetting simple things see your GP in private and explain your concerns. The usual route in the UK is to refer you for help if you agree, and GP's can also refer you to the secondary mental health service. Your mental health can then be assessed and treated. This also opens up many avenues for additional help, such as a domestic abuse support worker. Please use these services, they are not there to penalize or mistreat you, they are there to help so be open with them.

The most obvious impact of domestic abuse is physical injury, it has been recorded that 70% of domestic abuse injuries to the victim are physical, domestic abuse was also linked to a number of health problems in the Crisp & Stanko 2001 study, including sexually transmitted infections (STD's), unwanted pregnancies, irritable bowel syndrome, and gynecological problems. Abuse, in general, is the most prevalent cause of depression and mental health difficulties in women. This can and often does lead to victims self-harming and/or attempting suicide. In a study in 1996 by Stark & Flitcraft, 33% of women attending accident and emergencies for self-harm had experienced domestic abuse and it was noted that women who have experienced domestic abuse are five times more likely to attempt suicide. Both genders can and do suffer abuse. Current trends and surveys show that men are more likely to commit abuse against women, and women are more likely to report this abuse.

Survivors of domestic abuse could have been in toxic relationships for years or decades without actually realizing it. They are often diagnosed with a 'generalized anxiety disorder' or/and depression and trauma. These are serious mental health disorders and the symptoms are very broad and different for everyone.

Claire's law

It's perfectly normal to want to know more when you're buying a new house or new car, after all they are VERY important objects in your life and you wouldn't just take the past owner's words on their condition! You would look into their past and possibly even pay a third-party specialist for their evaluation. These laws cannot be used as a form of control or harassment as the Police carry out their own risk assessments and alongside other safeguarding agencies, will consider whether any information disclosure is legal, necessary, and proportionate. Remember only 23% to 35% of domestic abuse is reported and only around 5% of these lead to convictions. It's better to be safe, not sorry. Why then are some so scared to look into the past of a new partner, especially when things are starting to get serious and you're considering the next steps. There are ways to do this, for both domestic abuse and in relation to safeguarding your children. Everyone has bad traits and red flags will pop up from time to time, if you or a friend gets concerned you can do one of two things. Ask them outright, or look into their past. With both of the following, you will need their names, date of birth, previous names, address, and previous addresses if known. Please understand any disclosure is normally in person at a police station or at your home. If they do have a record, you will be given information to enable you to make an informed choice of your future together. If they have no record then the request could be stopped at any time by the police and you would be informed. The Domestic Violence Disclosure Scheme is known as 'Clare's Law' in the UK, an initiative named after 36-year-old Clare Wood who was murdered by her boyfriend in 2009. Its aim is to protect people from domestic abuse. You have the right to ask the police whether a current partner represents a risk of violence. Others such as concerned third parties, parents, friends, etc can also apply. If the police have information that may impact the safety of that person they will inform them.

Normally this process should take around 15-35 days. If there are serious concerns or a crime has been reported during the reporting process then the police will act quickly. If just information is needed because you have been with an abuser in the past then asking these questions should NOT be an issue to your partner. If they get angry and start to threaten you, make you 'feel' bad for not trusting them, then that is cause to worry and even more cause for checking them out. You can start a Claire's Law by contacting the police (United Kingdom). They will ask your reasons and if any crime has been committed as well as if the person you are asking about knows you are asking for this information and how they might react if they find out.

"You are never obliged to accept abuse from anyone, friends, family, or partner."

Sarah's Law

This is another type of disclosure program but aimed towards child sex offenses. If your new partner is going to have access to your children and you have concerns, this law allows anyone to formally ask the police if they have any child sexual offenses. Some police authorities have online forms you can fill in, otherwise, you can ring 101 and ask them to make a request under Sarah's law. Normally the information is only given to a parent or carer and any information given must be kept confidential as legal action could be taken if the information is disclosed to anyone else.

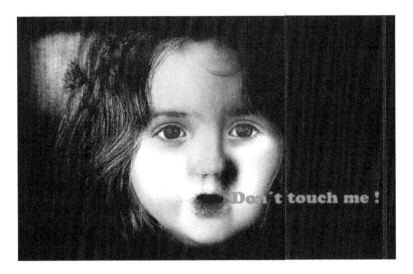

The following sections will give you a basic knowledge of recognizing the signs of mental and emotional abuse. Please take each section slowly and discuss with your volunteer or support worker. Remember Abuse is a scale, it's important to talk through your experiences with a professional to fully understand abuse.

Negative Reinforcement

Negative reinforcement in this concept (used by an abuser) simply uses verbal reassurances, manipulation, or lies to strengthen (reinforce) the idea or outcome the perpetrator wants and in doing so, convinces you that their way is the best or only way to avoid a negative outcome (**Aversive Stimuli**).

Aversive Stimuli

In psychology, aversives are unpleasant stimuli that induce changes in behavior via negative reinforcement or positive punishment. By applying an aversive immediately before or after a behavior the likelihood of the target behavior occurring in the future is reduced. Aversives can vary from being slightly unpleasant or irritating to physically, psychologically and/or emotionally damaging. It is not the level of unpleasantness or intention that matter, but rather the level of effectiveness the unpleasant event has on changing (decreasing) behavior that defines something as aversive.

Abusers can expertly reinforce beliefs and convince you that some type of discomfort, either physical or psychological will be avoided by following their idea. If you follow their instructions you will avoid the nasty consequences.

The type of influence an abuser has can be quite difficult to expose. Examples can be a great way to get a better idea of how someone can influence your beliefs.

Consider the following examples:

- In order to avoid sunburn, you are told to use sunscreen.

- You make a mess and are told to clean it up to avoid an argument

- You leave the house early to avoid getting stuck in traffic and being late for work.

- Someone is a terrible cook, but are constantly telling you how good they are and how good there food tastes.

All these examples avoid negative outcomes by influencing you into performing a specific behavior or action. Most are good but abusers use the same tactics to convince you to do things or think things their way, rather than distorting the truth as in gaslighting (Page 39).

One of the best ways to understand this behavior is to think of it as something being subtracted from the situation to give a better outcome for the abuser, not yourself.

Examples of reinforcing influence in abuse;

- Telling you how you need to give the abuser money to 'prevent' something bad from happening.

- Telling you to behave in a certain way in front of others to prevent them from not liking you,

- Telling you to hurt someone or attack someone to teach them a lesson and respect you.

- Shifting a negative focus away from them to you - such as if the police want to question the abuser but they instead tell you to lie for them or you will be in trouble instead or lose your children, the house or your family.

- Someone new wants to be your friend or help you, but your partner doesn't like them so consistently tells you how bad they are, using methods such as your always upset around them, they are planning something bad, only after your money, trying to steal you away from them.

- They constantly tell you that you are controlling, but are themselves monitoring your whereabouts and phone at all times.

- They keep telling you they care for you and you should not be out late - but in reality they like to control you and are using this as an excuse. The constant talk about it is reinforcing that belief.

Quotes for reflection

"I was afraid to have knives in the house, I knew when she was in a temper, there would be no second-guessing and no remorse afterward! I knew I would simply be gone"
- Anonymous

"do not look for healing at the feet of those who broke you"
— Rupi Kaur, Milk, and Honey

"Arguments would last for hours or days, often over the smallest thing. A wet cloth on the sink, a slight glance at the opposite sex, or a simple human mistake"
- Anonymous

"Of pain, you could wish only one thing: that it should stop. Nothing in the world was so bad as physical pain. In the face of pain, there are no heroes."
—George Orwell, 1984

"In every single argument, the cause of it was ignored and every single thing I had ever done wrong was bought into it. I found myself apologizing again and again for things I never really understood and I was constantly walking on eggshells afraid to bring up anything which needed discussing in case it ended badly"
- Anonymous

"In order to escape accountability for his crimes, the perpetrator does everything in his power to promote forgetting. If secrecy fails, the perpetrator attacks the credibility of his victim. If he cannot silence her absolutely, he tries to make sure no one listens."
— Judith Lewis Herman, Trauma and Recovery: The Aftermath of Violence – From Domestic Abuse to Political Terror

"Often it isn't the initiating trauma that creates seemingly insurmountable pain, but the lack of support after."
— S. Kelley Harrell, Gift of the Dreamtime - Reader's Companion

"You can recognize survivors of abuse by their courage. When silence is so very inviting, they step forward and share their truth so others know they aren't alone."
— Jeanne McElvaney, Healing Insights: Effects of Abuse for Adults Abused as Children

"Shouldn't there be more distaste in our mouths for the abusers than for those who continue to love the abusers?"
— Colleen Hoover, It Ends with Us

"Nobody has ever killed themselves over a broken arm. But every day, thousands of people kill themselves because of a broken heart. Why? Because emotional pain hurts much worse than physical pain."
— Oliver Markus Malloy, Bad Choices Make Good Stories (Omnibus): How The Great American Opioid Epidemic of The 21st Century Began - a Memoir

"Memories demand attention and these memories will have teeth."
— C. Kennedy, Slaying Isidore's Dragons

"You can recognize survivors by their creativity. In soulful, insightful, gentle, and nurturing creations, they often express the inner beauty they brought out of childhood storms."
— Jeanne McElvaney, Childhood Abuse: Tips to Change Child Abuse Effects

"One of the best ways of repressing emotions is artificial certainty."
— Stefan Molyneux

"It is a rare person who can cut himself off from mediate and immediate relations with others for long spaces of time without undergoing a deterioration in personality."
— Harry Stack Sullivan, The Interpersonal Theory of Psychiatry

"Instead of saying, "I'm damaged, I'm broken, I have trust issues," say "I'm healing, I'm rediscovering myself, I'm starting over."
— Horacio Jones

"Survivors of abuse show us the strength of their personal spirit every time they smile."
— Jeanne McElvaney, Healing Insights: Effects of Abuse for Adults Abused as Children

"In situations of captivity, the perpetrator becomes the most powerful person in the life of the victim, and the psychology of the victim is shaped by the actions and beliefs of the perpetrator."
— Judith Lewis Herman, Trauma and Recovery: The Aftermath of Violence – From Domestic Abuse to Political Terror

"It is strange... the reasons one feels he doesn't deserve things."
— C. Kennedy, Slaying Isidore's Dragons

"In order to believe clients' accounts of trauma, you need to suspend any preconceived notions that you have about what is possible and impossible in human experience. As simple as they may sound, it may be difficult to do so."
— Aphrodite Matsakis, Post-Traumatic Stress Disorder

"If the abuser is a parent or caretaker, the abuse may be the most attention the child has had from that person. To the child, withholding attention can be a powerful form of coercion. Sexual molestation may be accompanied by physical expressions of affection that are sometimes the only affection the child receives."
— Rick Moskovitz, Lost in the Mirror: An Inside Look at Borderline Personality Disorder

"Walking away from someone you love is not an immoral thing. If that person isn't good for your wellbeing in any way, it's important to step away from that relationship."
— Arien Smith

"People expect all stories of abuse to be loud and angry but they're not. Sometimes they're quiet and cruel and swept under the rug."
— Trista Mateer, Aphrodite Made Me Do It

"Over the years, I had come to understand many things, but one was the clearest of all: you can survive anything if only you have one true friend."
— Meara O'Hara, The Wanderess and her Suitcase

"I thought that the world did not want me, but the truth was that I did not want myself."
— M.M. van der Reijden, Winter Magnolia

"The reason why you need emotional support is because it's important for survivors to be heard. To be understood. To be able to express yourself without fearing criticism or harsh judgment. To be validated for your pain, suffering, and loss. For others to be there for you to encourage you, especially if you're having a bad day or feeling triggered."
— Dana Arcuri, Soul Cry: Releasing & Healing the Wounds of Trauma

"My pain has always deserved a voice and I will not deny it, but I won't devote my life to it either."
— Trista Mateer, Aphrodite Made Me Do It

Help is available.

(Correct at time of publishing, UK)

Victim Support: 08081689111 – www.victimsupport.org.uk
A national charity dedicated to helping anyone affected by
crime – not just victims and witnesses, but friends, family
and anyone else caught up in the aftermath.
Rape Crisis: 08088029999 – www.rapecrisis.org.uk
A national charity offering confidential help, advice and a
range of Rape Crisis Centres around the UK.
Galop: 08009995428 – www.galop.org.uk A national charity
providing advice and support to members of the LGBT
community.
Survivors UK: 02035983898 – www.survivorsuk.org A
national charity supporting men who have been raped or
sexually assaulted.
Crimestoppers: 0800555111 – www.crimestoppers-uk.org
A national charity with a free helpline for reporting crime
anonymously.
Refuge: 08082000247 – www.refuge.org.uk Refuge
supports women, children and men with a range of services,
including refuges, independent advocacy, community
outreach and culturally specific services.
Women's Aid: www.womansaid.org.uk Women's aid is a
national charity working to end domestic abuse against
women and children.
Men's Advice Line: 08088010327 –
www.mensadviceline.org.uk Confidential helpline for men
experiencing domestic violence.
BeAbuseAware: www.beabuseaware.org – free resources and
information for victims of domestic abuse.

If you are in an abusive relationship or someone you know
is, seek help. Call the police if you or someone you know is
in immediate danger, or your National Domestic Abuse
helpline. Learning what help is available, and how to access
it can save someone's life.

About the Author

Stephen Cooke is an abuse survivor and a trained Gas engineer with other qualifications including Computing, business, law and abuse recognition. This book, What is abuse is the first in a series of books dealing with domestic abuse from the perspective of a survivor.

Having met his first partner in approximately 1996, Stephen who was studying computer science and hoping for a career in microchip development was constantly hiding the scars and scratches from physical attacks he sustained. Unfortunately due to growing up in a working single parent household, Stephen's experience of family life was quite isolated and believed it when told this behavior was normal. In fact this behavior was also shown within her immediate family. Hostility, fights and abuse were rampant in their closed social environment. It was commonplace to be physical, emotionally abusive and make threats on an almost daily basis.

Stephen was later subjected to isolation tactics and married in a small ceremony to avoid any fights or drama which were normal in or after family gatherings. His ex partner would often blame external influences on her rages and outright unbelievable behavior. Mentally degrading, assaults and name-calling were commonplace and serious arguments happened 3-4 times a week. These were often blamed directly on her depression, her family or friends who were 'stirring the pot'. Her aggression I can only compare to that of a narcissist, although this was never officially confirmed due to her consistent lying. Stephen was fired from one of his jobs due to having to keep coming home to reassure his wife and calm down her rages. She completely refused to seek help, and unfortunately her family would back her up, saying blood is thicker than water, even knowing she was in the wrong.

In 2015, Stephen suffered stage 3 head and neck cancer. This along with now staying trapped and isolated with an abuser at home left him with serious memory drops where he would be left confused and almost completely helpless. After this, Stephen had to retire from his profession as a Gas Engineer. Trapped with an abuser, no way out, no one to help and reliant on her. Stephen, being unaware of the fact his home life was domestic abuse, coupled with his confusion and short term memory loss attempted to take his own life.

After this, he started to reach out and made contact with other victims. They made him aware of what was happening and helped him cope mentally. In 2018, after a prolonged period of abuse Stephen separated from his partner but stayed living together (for the children!). During the 2 years of cohabiting, Stephen had to move into the conservatory so he could physically lock the door away from her rages and aggression. During this time he called the police a number of times due to her physical and mental abuse, which had also shifted quite dramatically towards the children. But nothing was ever done. Stephen, unfortunately discovered the system, as well as some individuals were quite ignorant of abuse towards males.

Then in May 2020, after witnessing his daughter and how the abuse was directly affecting her, asked his ex wife to leave. She did and things remained somewhat 'ok' for a few weeks. But after his wife got others to start abusing their son, Stephen had cut off all contact for their safety and told her to seek a child arrangement order so safeguarding protections could be put in place. Stephen got full custody and contact with their mother was left to the discretion of the children due to there age. His ex wife decided to call the police after Stephen safeguarded the children, claiming the very things she was doing. The police then immediately arrested him. This was unfounded and again Stephen witnessed first hand the bias of the system towards males. Stephen was not even allowed to report her to the police for domestic abuse, because she had reported him first.

Stephen now focuses his time helping victims of domestic abuse, raising awareness on all types of abuse and boundaries after trauma. This he does with the continued support of his friends and family, even though he still suffers with mind drops, which are triggered by his traumatic past or any type of 'drama' with his ex wife. Stephen runs the website www.beabuseaware.org and offers free resources and information to victims of domestic abuse.

To this day his ex wife has no 'official' record of any type linking her to being a perpetrator of abuse. Stephen's opinion in cases where the perpetrator cannot be identified for whatever reason, is that both parties should have details stored on the police national computer to allow for information sharing and Clare's Law requests.

Thank you to the following for the use of their free images and clip-art and to all the online resources who offer free information and advice on the identification of abuse.

clipartsworld.com
@journey_to_wellness_
seekpng.com
clipartmax.com
Gograph.com
pixabay.com
freepik.com

Printed in Great Britain
by Amazon